The SERMON

The SERMON

Dancing the Edge of Mystery

EUGENE L. LOWRY ....

Abingdon Press
Nashville

THE SERMON: DANCING THE EDGE OF MYSTERY

Copyright © 1997 by Eugene L. Lowry

This book is printed on recycled, acid-free, elemental-chlorine–free paper.

Library of Congress Cataloging-in-Publication Data

Lowry, Eugene L.
    The sermon: dancing the edge of mystery/Eugene L. Lowry.
        p.   cm.
    Includes bibliographical references and index.
    ISBN 0-687-01543-X (alk. paper)
    1. Preaching.   2. Storytelling—Religious aspects—Christianity.
I. Title.
BV4211.2.L69   1997
251—dc21   97-6707
                                                                    CIP

Scripture quotations unless otherwise indicated, are from the New Revised Standard Version Bible, copyright © 1989 by the Division of Christian Education of the National Council of the Churches of Christ in the United States of America.

Scripture quotations noted RSV are from the Revised Standard Version of the Bible, copyright 1946, 1952, 1971 by the Division of Christian Education of the National Council of the Churches of Christ in the USA. Used by permission.

Scripture quotations noted JB are from The Jerusalem Bible, copyright © 1966 by Darton, Longman & Todd, Ltd. and Doubleday & Company, Inc. Used by permission of the publishers.

04 05 06 — 10 9 8 7 6 5

MANUFACTURED IN THE UNITED STATES OF AMERICA

For
The Academy of Homiletics

PREFACE

*T*he book is dedicated to my professional family—those colleagues who have become community—namely The Academy of Homiletics. What a marvelous professional guild—shaped by the combination of remarkable diversity and crucial mutual respect. It is a challenging and undergirding community of scholars/teachers. For many of us, it is home. I am grateful.

The Administration and Board of Trustees of Saint Paul School of Theology made sabbatical time possible for the completion of the work. David Buttrick allowed the use of his phrase "dancing the edge of mystery," which I hope names the sensibility with which I attempt to work. Sarah, best friend and spouse, has been patron to this project in all the wonderful and none of the problematic senses of the word. Shall we dance?

Eugene L. Lowry

CONTENTS

INTRODUCTION

For at least twenty-five years now, the discipline of North American homiletics has been in the throes of an emerging new homiletical paradigm. Many of us mark its beginning with the publication of Fred Craddock's first book on preaching—and with its first sentence: "We are all aware that in countless courts of opinion the verdict on preaching has been rendered and the sentence passed." That was 1971, and some of us remember well the mood toward preaching in those times. "All this slim volume asks," he continued, "is a stay of execution until one other witness be heard."[1]

That powerful slim volume ranged from biblical hermeneutics (how one works with a text) through the linguistics of theology (how one goes about understanding the gospel), to the preaching art (how one shapes the flow of ideas). Of particular concern to Craddock was the issue of the relationship of preacher and congregation. He insisted that the congregation was "deserving [of] the right to participate"[2] in the sermonic trip and not just be let in on the destination.

Well, the world's court of opinion listened.

Elsewhere I once suggested that Craddock kicked in a door that cannot now be closed. Given the current wrestling with postmodern thought—as well as a reappraisal of the "eclipse of biblical narrative"[3]—I think it fair to say the hinges are no longer on the door. Some would aver that the draft through that open door is not only brisk but even unnecessarily unsettling. Many others consider it a refreshing gale.

Perhaps the beginning of what Richard Eslinger called the "Copernican Revolution" in North American homiletics[4] could be dated with an earlier publication: *Design for Preaching* (1958), by H. Grady Davis. It was he who by means of free verse introduced a new metaphor for preaching when he said, "A sermon is like a tree."[5]

For many of us, that was the first time we had heard sermons compared with some form of organic life. After hearing for years about *constructing, assembling, building,* and *putting together* sermons, the metaphoric tease of the term *tree* changed everything. And that was almost forty years ago!

A lot has happened since then. The "New Homiletic," as it is often called, has evoked new images and new definitions about what preaching is all about—with such terms as *inductive* preaching, *phenomenological* sermons, *story*telling, *eyewitness* biblical accounts, and *narrative* plots.

These terms all suggest a common homiletical family, but they are not genetic clones. Some members of the clan don't even claim their own kin. Nor should this new family be cut off in either-or fashion from the larger tradition. After twenty-five years of fertile flurry, it is time to look more closely into genetic links, apparent resemblances, and, especially, family differences.

With very serious questions being raised these days about the rationalism of the Enlightenment, and Romanticism's assumption about universal human experience, a central issue that needs attention is the fundamental question about the goal of a sermon. What do we believe about preaching? What is its purpose? What happens, anyway? Are the terms *preaching* and *proclamation* synonymous, or quite different in meaning? And how might we speak about truth?

If a sermon is in some fundamental sense similar to the life of a tree, then *time, growth,* and *sequence* take on new meaning. What might that be? And how best, then, does a preacher prepare to effect some kind of evocative performance—particularly in light of multiple needs, diverse texts, and even polyvalent parables?

If preaching is less an architectural science and more a horticultural art, how can we learn to do it? Surely, this question of praxis is central. If a sermon is "like a tree," how do I hone my pruning skills? Is this new paradigm only for a strange few, or is this homiletical shift into the new century a broad and sweeping movement? How *might* I, *should* I, *can* I relate to these fundamental issues being raised?

Theologically speaking—and particularly given this remarkable time and place of transition—how does one go about "dancing the edge of mystery"?[6]

1

H. Grady Davis and Fred Craddock are not the only voices impelling the paradigm shift in North American homiletics. With differing points of entry, various agenda, and diverse goals—even fascinating disagreements—a number of homiletical writers are shaping the new day.

In metaphoric terms, we have not only Davis's *tree* and Craddock's *trip,* but also R. E. C. Browne's *gesture,* Tom Troeger's *music of speech,* David Buttrick's *move,* Henry Mitchell's *celebration,* Lucy Rose's *conversation,* David Schlafer's *play,* and Paul Scott Wilson's *spark of imagination*—as well as my *plot,* of course!

What is at stake here can be identified as

> *how we handle biblical texts,*
> *with what theological assumptions and convictions,*
> *resulting in what kinds of sermonic shapes*
> *toward what particular homiletical goals.*

Among other things.

Perhaps the best way to begin is to assess quickly—very quickly—some of the central issues that have given rise to our particular time and place. David Buttrick's pointed illustration of "worn-out preaching conventions" will serve us well.

"Many preachers," he states, "were trained to speak from one-verse texts"—even including some preachers within lectionary-based traditions. "If we did not preach from snippets of scripture, we operated with what might be described as a method of distillation."[7] He explains by reference to the Lukan passage about the centurion who had heard of Jesus and through emissaries begged Jesus to come to his house to heal his stricken slave—but then felt unworthy for Jesus to enter the house and, hence, pleaded for Jesus to just "say the word" (Luke 7:2-10 RSV).

Notes Buttrick:

> Usually . . . [the preacher] approaches the passage as if it were objectively "there," a static construct from which . . . [one] may get some-*thing* to preach on. [The preacher] . . . either . . . will grab one of the verses—"Say the word," "I am not worthy," "he loves our nation, and he built us our synagogue"—treating the verse as a topic, or . . . will distill some general theme from the passage, for example, "the intercession of friends," "the compassion of Jesus," "an example of humility." Notice, in either case the preacher treats the passage as if it were a still-life picture in which some*thing* may be found, object-like to preach on. What has been ignored? The composition of the "picture," the narrative structure, the movement of the story, the whole question of what in fact the *passage* may want to preach. Above all, notice that the passage has been treated as a stopped, objective picture from which something may be taken out to preach on![8]

This process of distillation "developed in the eighteenth century with the rise of rationalism," observes Buttrick—partly as a way to "cheerfully sidestep the embarrassments of the biblical miracle." Indeed the method "parodied scientific method."[9] By the second half of the twentieth century, the "method of distillation" was still very much alive in the pulpits of North America. A lot of us were raised on its diet.

Buttrick is not the only one to raise serious questions about biblical hermeneutical principles that many of us have absorbed from a previous generation of preachers and—perhaps until recently—have simply taken for granted. Particularly in the area of parable studies, such scholars as Norman Perrin, John Dominic Crossan, and Dan Otto Via have opened new doors for preachers by raising important questions that are wonderfully stimulating and radical.

In the context of *narrative* biblical hermeneutics, Hans Frei has provided the most classic form of this concern. Although his groundbreaking volume *The Eclipse of Biblical Narrative* was written more than twenty years ago, it seems to be cited more now in homiletical literature than ever before.

Frei's concerns centered precisely on this issue on the separation of biblical content and form. As he put it, the Scripture "simultaneously . . . depicts and renders the reality . . . of what it talks about."[10] So the split happened, the "great reversal" in which, unfortunately, the biblical story was made to fit "into another world with another story rather than incorporating that world into the biblical story."[11] (Which is precisely what the imagined preacher in Buttrick's example wound up doing.) The texts, explains Mark Ellingsen, "are emptied of their own reality, and treated only as symbolic expressions of . . . [an allegedly] deeper truth."[12]

From the vantage point of the African American homiletical tradition, Henry Mitchell observes, "White preaching . . . [tends to focus on] the production of a stimulating idea."[13] He suggests that "feelings in [white] Western culture have somehow been declared unworthy," but that "black culture of the masses has not progressed to the level of this lofty and ancient mistake." Mitchell theorizes further that "the earlier Greek dichotomy of flesh and spirit was perhaps only made worse by the Enlightenment, which added reason-vs.-feeling to the division of the human psyche."[14]

What I believe has happened in these last twenty-five years of homiletical theory is that numerous newer voices have picked up on the creative cues of such writers as H. Grady Davis and R. E. C. Browne, and have begun rethinking our homiletical assumptions and convictions. It is as though Craddock's book gave permission to explore. In similar fashion, and reaching a bit farther back in time, Thomas Long has provided another accounting for "this shift in contemporary preaching."[15]

"Once upon a time," he suggests:

> Homiletics (the theological study of preaching) and rhetoric (the art of effective speaking) were a happily married couple. From Augustine's *On Christian Doctrine* . . . all the way to the big, systematic homiletical textbooks in vogue in the nineteenth century, Christian homiletics looked to the Bible and to theology for the *content* of sermons and then to the rules and fashions of classical rhetoric for the *form* and *style* of sermons.

Long labels it a "mixed marriage—homiletics being Jewish and rabbinical in background . . . ; rhetoric being Greek." Calling it a marriage of convenience, Long avers: "Homileticians knew what preachers were supposed to say, and rhetoricians knew how they were to say it, so that listeners could hear it and be persuaded by it." To make a long story short, Long asserts that unfortunately, the marriage "was doomed" by rhetoric's illness—having suffered a "Barth Attack."[16]

Certainly, Barth would have little use for such a marriage because of his denial of natural revelation's affirmation of the human capacity to know God. As Long concludes the matter: "Rhetorical issues were not merely secondary concerns to Barth; they were to be eliminated from homiletical method for epistemological reasons."[17]

Is it any wonder that when New Testament scholar Fred Craddock was called to teach both New Testament *and* preaching, such hermeneutical, theological, and communicational matters were at the heart of his work?

Craddock's initial writing, hence, focused on the homiletical bottom line of these inherited hermeneutical and theological traditions. In particular, he noted the usual deductive shape that resulted from such a mind-set. He called it "packaged conclusions,"[18] that in a markedly authoritarian manner get dropped on the listeners of a congregation, which "if . . . on the team . . . [serves] as javelin catcher."[19]

Craddock's work has always emphasized the necessity for unity of substance and form. It wasn't simply principles of good communication that prompted his proposal for inductive preaching methodology; it actually centered on his work as a biblical scholar. Says Craddock, "Exegesis is inductive if it is healthy and honest. . . . If exegesis has to labor under the burden of providing particular support for a dogmatic conclusion already occupying one's mind, it ceases to be exegesis."[20]

My entrance into the homiletical conversation was prompted by my concern for the sermon's sequential form. Agreeing with Craddock about the centrality of the matter of movement, I found it obvious that whether one is taking a trip or hearing a joke, *anticipation* is key. Hence, the sermon ought to move from "expectation to fulfillment."[21]

Although by analogy Craddock drew the principle of anticipation from biblical exegetical work, my connection surely came implicitly from music. Stephen Crites is right that "the rhythm and melody lines of music are inherently temporal," which by means of a "succession of pulses and pitched vibrations" provide the listener with a "unity through time."[22]

It became increasingly clear to me that when sermons were really heard, they were sermons that moved from *itch to scratch*. Moreover, this principle is true not occasionally, or with certain biblical texts and not others, or on only some occasions, but always (with the caveat that the saints will, of course, listen always—that's why we call them saints).

Thus, the notion of a sermon as a *narrative plot* has become central to my work. And by the term *narrative* I do not mean *story* as such. (But we are ahead of ourselves; more about narrative and story later.)

Another concern of our time and place ought to be added to biblical hermeneutical, theological, and rhetorical issues already named. Or is it that a central ingredient to the above-mentioned concerns is a noteworthy thread running through them? The issue is *time*—with temporality, with narrativity itself, indeed with the facticity of historical existence.

Time "is the way we live the world"[23] claimed Frederick Jameson. It is, according to Thomas Mann, "the medium of life."[24] Believing that temporality is a universal condition of human existence, Crites declares that "the formal quality of experience through time is inherently narrative."[25] Terrence Tilley agrees by noting that "human experience . . . [is] *inherently durational*".[26]

Indeed, Lonnie D. Kliever is convinced that "the impact of a story is not limited to the life exemplified or the principle illustrated in the story. Stories have the power to shape life because they formally embody the shape of life."[27]

After citing my statement that "a sermon is an ordered form of moving time,"[28] Richard Eslinger goes on to explain the potential consequences for preaching, that

> ideas, propositions, thematics—all of these have a spatial quality; we were conditioned to speaking of "building the sermon" through

outlines, points and theme sentences. But if, however, human experience is inherently temporal, a homily will be designed to shape experience rather than to assemble thoughts.[29]

(This was not Eslinger's final view in this writing, however, due to the influence of George Lindbeck's "cultural-linguistic" model.)

What is important to note for now is that when Buttrick properly complains about the "process of distillation," time, story, narrativity, and temporality are removed from the proper equation. And the eclipse of biblical narrative that Frei warned us about is that unwarranted reversal that attempts to suck meaning out of the narrative in which it lives. Craddock's concern for a process of discovery to replace homiletical announcements of ideational conclusions is based on a profound understanding of the importance of sequence. In my construal of narrative preaching, time is central to the homiletical event.

In "Preaching as the Creation of an Experience: the Not-So-Rational Revolution of the New Homiletic," Robert Reid, Jeffrey Bullock, and David Fleer focus their essay on "the New Homiletic, the emerging Protestant paradigm for preaching, with particular attention to theorists Craddock, Buttrick, Mitchell, and Lowry." Their claim is that "the creation of an experience in which both speaker and audience are co-participants in an event of understanding" is the central focus "that marks the productive unity of this paradigm shift in homiletic method."[30] Well, we shall see.

The Current Shape of the New Homiletic

"The times they are a-changing,"[31] says David Buttrick. "What kind of homiletic do we frame for the forming new age?"[32] However one defines the issues that have brought us here—and they are many—we have come to a new day, a new paradigm in preaching. "Not since the Middle Ages or the Reformation," declares Paul Scott Wilson, "have such mighty winds swept the homiletical highlands."[33]

How now do we define the new modalities of the preaching art? First, we have to choose a category in which to work in naming the changes. Lucy Rose has named four basic homiletical categories—four central variables in preaching: (1) the *purpose* of preaching, (2) the *content* of preaching, (3) the *language* of preaching, and (4) the *form* of preaching.[34] These four variables are all interconnected. One can enter the door of any of the four and wind up engaging the other three. It is inevitable. Which door shall we choose to enter? By calling the new homiletical paradigm "transformational preaching," Rose has settled on the *purpose* of preaching as the defining category.[35]

On the other hand, Eslinger, in naming the five "living options in homiletic method" (story, narrative in the black tradition, narrative and the sermonic plot, the inductive method, and a phenomenological method), has chosen the *form* of a sermon as the key. Reid and others (above) said *producing experience* was the proper context for definition.

I choose *form* or *shape* as the most helpful defining category in describing several current versions of the new homiletic. Not that *shape* is more important than *purpose, language,* or *content,* nor that shape is the only category of significant difference. Far from it.

Indeed, there are significant—even radical—shifts of thought regarding both the purpose and the content of preaching. (We will spend a chapter on each.) I simply think focusing briefly on sermonic shape as the defining category is the most economical way to name the commonalities and differences.

One of the things we will observe very quickly about the "new" homiletic is that many of its forms have quite long histories. Their newly appropriated identity and purpose in the context of our time and place—together with their interconnections—give credibility to the adjective *new.* It has been suggested that what makes this paradigm shift noteworthy is in its turning to homiletical patterns and convictions that had been abandoned or marginalized by modernity. Reid wonders if this moment might just represent "the recovery of a premodern paradigm."[36]

Given the plurality of voices of the "new homiletic," we need to name six identifiable types or models—all related and all different. (And we will be quick about it.) Only then can we proceed with clarity to figure out where we are and how we can move forward. We will start with Craddock's model.

1. The Inductive Sermon

Craddock has enabled us to name and notice the consequences of ideational movement in any given sermon:

> Anyone who would preach effectively will have as . . . primary methodological concern the matter of movement. Does the sermon move and in what direction? . . . There are basically two directions in which thought moves: deductive and inductive. Simply stated, deductive movement is from the general truth to the particular application or experience while induction is the reverse. . . . In other words, . . . [in a deductive sermon] the conclusion precedes the development, a most unnatural mode of communication.[37]

He claims more than the compatibility of inductive preaching with honest biblical exegesis. "The plain fact of the matter is," he declares, that "everyone lives inductively, not deductively."[38] Moreover, "*how* one preaches is to a large extent *what* one preaches."[39] One's views on such crucial issues as revelation and authority get revealed by methodological choices. Inductive movement, believes Craddock, respects the integrity of the congregation and relates to the congregation as a corporate body. Induction not only generates interest, but assists sermonic unity, unlike deduction, which sometimes feels like "three sermonettes barely glued together."[40] Indeed, says Craddock, "the incarnation itself is the inductive method."[41]

2. The Story Sermon

This sermon type consists of a story told. (It may even be two stories told.) It may be a biblical account or it may be a contemporary parable, but it is fundamentally the telling of a story.

Among the writers in our time who are known as advocates of this type of preaching are Richard Jensen (*Telling the Story* and *Thinking in Story*) and Charles Rice, Edmund Steimle, and Morris Niedenthal (*Preaching the Story* and Rice in *The Embodied Word*). When the lawyer asked Jesus a question about how to identify a neighbor, Jesus preached a brief story sermon.

For purposes of definition, the story form is the easiest type to describe. This does not mean that it is an easy type to understand.

For example, many critics (and a few friends) see story as a thoroughly right-brain activity. Often that is true, but not always. It depends on the teller, the purpose, the listeners, the context, and the setting—as well as the content itself.

Particularly confusing for some is the question of definitional language for this form. Often the terms *story* and *narrative* are perceived as synonymous. Sometimes that is correct. The *story* of the rich young ruler, the *parable* of the rich young ruler, and the *narrative* of the rich young ruler, obviously, are all the same. Often biblical narrative criticism concerns the exploration of specific biblical stories. But not always. One might speak of the canon as one overarching *narrative* in shape without meaning the *story* of the canon.

Technically, the term *narrative* means a "story" and a "teller." Which is quite appropriate—sometimes. One might indeed notice that a story sermon is also an inductive sermon since it begins with particulars and makes its way to a conclusion of some kind. The difference is that in a story sermon, you have characters, setting, action, tone, and plot.

3. The Narrative Sermon

What identifies the usual narrative sermon most readily is its plot form, which always—one way or another—begins with a felt *discrepancy* or conflict, and then makes its way through *complication* (things always get worse), makes a decisively sharp turn or *reversal*, and then moves finally toward *resolution* or closure.

Such a sermon may involve a story told (in which case it would be better called a story sermon). Then again—and more likely—it may not involve any kind of story at all. In *Overhearing the Gospel*, in which the narrative type of sermon was featured, Craddock explained that

> by narrative structure I am not proposing . . . a long story or a series of stories or illustrations. While such may actually be the form used for a given message, it is not necessary in order to be narrative. Communication may be narrativelike and yet contain a rich variety of materials: poetry, polemic, anecdote, humor, exegetical analysis, commentary.[42]

Which ought to make our differential between the terms *story* and *narrative* clear.

However, given the fact that some writers in the field are still confusing the terms, it might be helpful by analogy to note the similarity yet difference between other related terms, such as *medicine* (as found in a prescription bottle) and the same yet different term *medicine* (as in the physician's vocation). This is a helpful analogy, it seems to me, because the physician's practice of *medicine* may call for the doctor to prescribe some *medicine*. Likewise, a *narrative* preacher may feel called upon to tell a *story* (to use a particular *narrative* within the *narrative* sermon). Again, a *character* in a play has a definable quality called *character*—which in this case may turn out to be quite a *character*.

Enough.

Toni Craven, professor of Hebrew Bible, has sorted these terms quite well—with her conclusion that the term *temporal sequencing* serves best and may refer either to *source* (narrative text) or to *presentation* (narrative discourse).[43]

Central, then, to what defines a narrative sermon is *sequence.* As Rose articulates it, although "the story sermon is a sermon that tells a story, the narrative sermon is a sermon that follows the sequential elements of a plot."[44]

One basic aspect of these first three types of preaching—inductive, story, and narrative—is a "strategic delay . . . [in arriving at] the preacher's meaning."[45] It will be important to keep alive this notion of "strategic delay" as we continue our exploration of related forms.

4. *The Transconscious African American Sermon*

This type of sermon gets its name from a term utilized by Henry Mitchell as a way of explaining the function of "communally stored wisdom and cultural affinity" that is central to African American homiletic experience. It names a form of knowing that lies just beneath the threshold of consciousness and that provides the glue to the congregational bond. "The art of Black preaching," says Mitchell, "is not *less* than logical; it is logical on *more levels* or wave lengths."[47]

While on paper the sermon may even appear to be traditionally structured—moving from exegesis through interpretation toward application—something else is going on. There is a trans-conscious narrativity also happening. William B. McClain describes this narrative work as "slow and deliberate to a build-up. The path the preacher takes may be winding with a few detours, but always he or she is expected to be heading someplace and to take time getting there."[48] Evans Crawford speaks of the *"antici-patory* silence."[49] McClain recalls the advice given to preacher and professor Zan Holmes:

> Start low; go slow,
> Go high; strike fire.
> Sit down.[50]

Such determining ingredients as the "pattern [of] . . . rhetoric, repetition, rhythm, and rest,"[51] folk-based orality, and "eye-witness"[52] biblical stories all draw on transconscious connections and then move toward the culminating sermonic celebration. This narrative expectation is so basic and so compelling that people may tell the preacher to "take your time." "The final role of celebration," notes Mitchell, is a "fitting climax. . . . All else leads up to this climactic moment."[53]

5. *The Phenomenological Move Sermon*

This homiletical model is the work of David Buttrick and is intended to address precisely the issues raised here. This style of sermon consists of a sequence of five or six plotted ideational units culminating in the sermonic conclusion.

"How do we preach a [biblical] story?"[54] asks Buttrick, who after setting aside several options, including "telling a swell story,"[55] opts for "preaching in the mode of immediacy." He explains: "We do not talk about a story, or even tell a story, so much as imitate a consciousness hearing and reacting to a story."[56]

Or again, some texts suggest a "reflective mode." "Sermons in the reflective mode preach neither a text nor a topic, but, instead, they convey a patterned field of contemporary understanding in consciousness that has been produced by a passage,"[57] according to Buttrick.

In some cases the preacher begins not with a text but with a human situation—"relating experience to gospel rather than gospel to experience." Such sermons are called "preaching in the praxis mode." Such preaching "addresses persons *in* lived experience and, therefore, starts with a hermeneutic of lived experience."[58]

Buttrick is not always fond of the term *narrative*—once even castigating the "recent hoopla over 'narrative preaching.' "[59] Nonetheless he accepts the idea of a plot. "The word *plot*," he points out in *Homiletic*, "may be applied to all kinds of hermeneutical acts; it is not restricted to stories."[60] In another recent writing, he even wrote a section "The Concept of Plot," which indicates that "the notion of plot matches the 'style' of our cultural moment." Although he could accept the notion of narrative in dealing with the mode of immediacy, he concludes: "I stress the notion of plotted mobility rather than narrativity."[61]

Such "plotted mobility" or movement is central to his concerns—particularly in light of his understanding that our reading of the biblical text should focus not so much on what it *says*, but on the question "what is the passage trying to *do?*"[62]

Elsewhere I have said that "if you imagine a sermon as a string of pearls, Buttrick's primary focus is upon the pearls; my point of entry centers upon the string."[63] (After all, Buttrick's "moves" are really "stops." The real "moves," seems to me, are in between.)

Sensing the fundamental compatibility with his work relative to sermonic shape, I wonder what it might be about the term *narrative* that is problematic for Buttrick? Could it be that the referent for the term *narrative* and the referent for the term *story* are often the same referent in popular usage—and that the term *story* evokes in him the unacceptable connotations of the subjectivized, the privatized, and the psychologized?

Whatever the case may be, Buttrick's concerns about sermon shape are clearly centered on *mobility*—behavioral, plotted, sequence.

6. *The Conversational-Episodal Sermon*

If it seems as though this type of sermon may be more than one type, you may be correct. Yet, several significant factors in preaching seem often to be found together—in variant ways. The term *conversational* has to do both with relational factors between preacher and congregation, and with language style. The term *episodal* has to do with sermon shape.

Says Carol Norén: "Persuasion to a particular point of view and/or transmission of religious truths are not the goals of the preacher. Instead, preaching is a profound act of human connection and intimacy."[64] Indeed, the sermon "may resemble a small group discussion on a topic or text."[65]

Lucy Rose has named this kind of pulpit presentation "conversational preaching." She explains that "in conversational preaching the preacher and the congregation envision themselves as exploring together the mystery of the Word for the lives of the worshipers." They all "gather symbolically at the round table where there is no head and no foot."[66]

Noteworthy, also, is the "affinity," as Norén describes it, "between feminist/liberation hermeneutics and preaching by women in general . . . [in] the way both favor narrative/historical texts."[67] In addition, she comments that "women preachers . . . [are characterized by their use] of concrete analogy between the biblical context and the contemporary one."[68] Taken altogether, these components lend themselves nicely to a form of episodal preaching. Such preaching moves forward, yet does not establish a tightly linear monological form.

Having said this, I think it obvious that this kind of preaching is not practiced only by women. My colleague Tex Sample's sermons almost always consist of three vignettes presented without transitional glue—falling into place with a unity known only at the conclusion of the third vignette.

Indeed, I sometimes think that Fred Craddock at his best may be more episodal than inductive only. Although he is obviously working inductively, sometimes instead of the movement of thought traveling along a singular road gathering momentum as it moves toward conclusion, the sermon will lure the congregation first into a text, then into a supermarket, then into a pensive ideational reflection, across a second text, through a powerful image, and then finally arrive where we could not have guessed.

Is it possible that the conversational-episodal sermon is one type of a less linear inductive sermon, which is a certain form of a narrative sermon? What is particularly noticeable in all six members of this new homiletic family is that they all refuse to announce a conclusion in advance, all "keep the cat in the bag," all are mobile, moving sequenced forms, which involve a strategic delay of the preacher's meaning. In quite different ways, and yet related, they all involve some kind of *plot*.

Moving On. Now that I have suggested our present time and place in North American homiletic history, and have very briefly described several of the current options related to the new homiletic, it is time to move on (or is it to move more deeply?) into the pressing issues that need our consideration.

Remembering Lucy Rose's identification of four central variables in preaching—*purpose, content, language,* and *shape*—I believe it is time to engage each one of them. The problem is: what should come first? (Somehow, I look for the evidence of some plottable logic.) Frankly, I would prefer to move quickly to the issue of shape and to explore the "how to do it" questions, but at this moment in our journey we may need first to figure out what we will be attempting to shape.

Seems to me that if first we attempt to fashion a working definition of what we think is a sermon's appropriate goal or purpose, then we will better be able to imagine content and language appropriate to the act and art of preaching. The important issues being raised by postmodern thinking will be crucial for us—as we sort out the argument among the differing views.

Then we will be able to engage the critical issues basic to questions of shape—and after that, of course, consider the payoff issues of how to go about doing it.

2

TASK ·· **GOAL**

*S*o, what is the point, the purpose of all these various current options in the preaching art—these "mobile, moving sequential forms"? Actually, the question is broader yet. What is the purpose of any kind or shape or type of sermon? What happens—or should happen—or might happen—or ought to happen—or does in fact happen with what we call the sermon?

Paul Scherer is clear: "A meeting has to take place."[69] He senses a divine "relentless moving in upon our lives."[70] God "is not intent on sharing conceptual truth," Scherer explains. "That must come later. It is not some saving measure of information he wants to impart; it is himself he wants to bestow."[71] So, preaching is "recital."[72]

Or is the truth of the matter closer to Barbara Brown Taylor's view that while "every sermon is God's creation," it is also "the creation of the preacher and the congregation"?[73] "The task of the preacher," says Frederick Buechner, "is to hold up life to us, by whatever gifts he or she has of imagination, eloquence, simple candor, to create images of life through which we can somehow see into the wordless truth of our lives."[74]

"From the transaction we call revelation," Craddock tells us, "we understand and implement the transaction we call preaching."[75] And with the claim of Charles Rice that the fundamental intention of a sermon is to facilitate "an encounter,"[76] we have come full circle. Frankly, it is difficult to know where around the circle to stop.

Perhaps, first, it might be helpful to hear Lucy Rose's description of the differing purposes she believes are claimed by *traditional* preaching, *kerygmatic* preaching, and *transformational* preaching.[77] (In her writing she also proposes a fourth type of preaching: *conversational* preaching, which I have included here as a subset of the kind of preaching she has called transformational. In order to fit her line of reasoning, one would need to retitle the third category.)

By *traditional*, she intends the kind of preaching that a lot of us grew up with. Ideational transmission is its goal. Divine truth as given by revelation is understood to come basically in propositional form. The purpose of the sermon is rhetorically oriented persuasion that will prompt conviction on the part of the congregation. Rose cites James Cox's definition of the goal as "getting the message across."[78] Truth is key.

This preaching exists fairly high on the human nature barometer—believing that if the preaching exhibits reasonable clarity (note the root term *reason*) and sufficient force (rhetorically understood appeal), the "expression and the idea exactly correspond."[79]

Whether theologically liberal or conservative, the preacher can presume sufficient human capacity for responses of hearing and doing. After all, the gospel and human experience are seen as continuous.

Kerygmatic preaching—on the other hand—sees little evidence to presume such continuity. The Word spoken involves an inbreaking—an "encounter with God." The gospel is understood as discontinuous with human experience, according to this type of preaching. The preacher is the herald of another realm altogether. Says Buttrick, this view sees preaching as "reconstituting a 'salvation history' of revelatory events; basically preaching is understood as a transmission of past disclosures [of the mighty acts of God] to the present day."[80]

Barth once apologized for developing a sermon around the sinking of the *Titanic,* and lamented getting caught up in his sermons with the outbreak of World War I.[81] "Pastors . . . [should] aim . . . beyond the hill of relevance,"[82] he said. (By a strange irony Barth's high doctrine of preaching actually becomes low by his insistence that the Word is God's affair only; human agency disappears; our part is mere reiteration: "The word of God on the lips of a man is an impossibility; it does not happen. . . . [It is] God's act.")[83]

Whereas traditional preaching focuses on ideational *transmission*, kerygmatic preaching focuses on *mediation*. This is so because the sermon's revelatory nature is understood not as conveyance of linguistic ideation, but as encounter with the self-manifestation of God. Persuasive techniques are not nearly so important with kerygmatic preaching; faithful witness is. Language is seen as fallen—yet God may break through.

The kind of preaching Rose calls *transformational* is what some others have called the new homiletic. Terms most often associated with this kind of preaching are *event* and *encounter* (a somewhat different encounter from that imaged in kerygmatic style). The "power of performative language to shape human consciousness" (or to evoke a new orientation) is central to some versions of this kind of preaching. Variables such as metaphor, plot, induction, experience, and imagination are commonly discussed with this understanding of the preaching act. Evocation is key.

This point of view has emerged on the scene in the context of a significant shift in biblical study—from the strong emphasis on historical, form, and redaction criticism to narrative criticism, and in parable studies moving from the understanding that a parable has *one* point to the notion that a parable *is* a point.

Some commentators link transformative preaching style to postmodern thinking, but if that is true, the form of postmodernism is not the radical form—seems to me. Between the *skeptical* and the *affirmative* postmodernists (as Pauline Marie Rosenau would define things),[84] most I have read would be in the affirmative camp—or who in biblical narrative studies would be called revisionists.

Again, Lucy Rose, whose categories we are utilizing, would have difficulty in my choice of using only three of her four categories. Not that she doesn't have a sense of affinity with *transformative* kind of preaching. Indeed, she had named herself as within such a group in a previous writing.[85] Yet she no longer wants to focus on transforming. "Mutual edification" is a better way to speak of her category of *conversational* preaching.[86] My sense is that were we to use another label for transformative preaching, such as the new homiletic, her views would feel at home—with more in common than not.

Before moving further, however, an important caveat is in order (maybe two). All three homiletical categories include very diverse preachers and theorists. Some persons appear to be bridge people with feet on both sides of a historical shift—such as H. Grady Davis, Henry Mitchell, and even David Buttrick. Perhaps Rose's name should be added here.

For one thing, being named as belonging inside one categorical group may mean no more than that being placed within another category would be even more problematic. Hence, any categorization needs to be generally accurate and yet reasonably loose. Folks in each of these categories argue a lot—not just with those outside the boundary, but especially with those within it. Family disagreements can run deep, particularly if one wants on occasion to disown the others.

Moreover, it is always worth remembering that forcing similarities into tight packages of presumed unity is the backdrop behind stereotyping. Remarkable amounts of mischief happen, for instance, by means of categorical guilt by association. Then again, it is always an easy trick to place the greatest perceived weakness of the "opposition's" point of view at the very center of their case. All of which is something for those of us who are advocates of a point of view to keep in mind.

The importance of categories is considerable, however. They not only assist us in understanding the various views that come our way, but they also help us recognize, identify, and reflect on our behavior—ways of doing that we may not yet have noticed.

Does It Happen?

Granting the differing descriptions of what is intended by our preaching—*transmission* of truth for traditional preachers, *mediation* of God's address for the kerygma tie preachers and *evocation of experiential event* for the transformational preachers—does it happen? Always? Only sometimes? When, under which circumstances, does it happen?

Some there are in each of the categorical camps who are remarkably certain that it happens. For example, let us hear the great liberal "preaching as transmission" preacher Harry Emerson Fosdick offer it without reservation:

> The preacher's business is not merely to discuss repentance but to persuade people to repent . . . , not merely to talk about the available power of God to bring victory over trouble and temptation, but to send people out from their worship on Sunday with victory in their possession. A preacher's task is to create in his congregation the thing he is talking about.

> It was a great day when I began to feel sure that a sermon could be thus immediately creative and transforming. A good sermon is an engineering operation by which a chasm is bridged so that spiritual goods on one side . . . are actually transported into personal lives upon the other. . . . It need never fail to make a transforming difference in some lives.[87]

Out of the quite different tradition of *mediation* we hear the preacher's affirmation that "Christ and I are present in the Word." The preacher is Gustaf Wingren, who made it clear that "preaching is not just talk about a Christ of the past, but is a mouth through which the Christ of the present offers us life today. In the Word we become partakers of that which took place and of that which shall take place."[88]

Agreeing with Fosdick and Wingren, but for differing reasons and goals, David Buttrick, too, is certain that it happens. In *Homiletic*, he asserts, "Preaching is the 'Word of God' in that it participates in God's purpose, is initiated by Christ, and is supported by the Spirit with community in the world."[89] Earlier in that book he writes, "Preaching constructs in consciousness a 'faith-world' related to God." As a result, "at minimum, preaching alters identity."[90] Stated another way: "What happens in preaching is that our world is transformed."[91]

In fact, he seems to know exactly when it does *not* happen: "Understand that *every* sentence that splits between a number and a content will disappear from consciousness the instant it is spoken."[92] Again, "*all* doublet sentences will delete."[93] (At least my computer asks if it's all right.)

Actually, all this is quite peculiar, because there is another side of Buttrick to which we will refer shortly. This other side of his thought wonders about mystery and observes how "we can wander into Presence."[94] Indeed, "false prophets," he believes, "are always those who have forgotten how to tremble in the presence of the Mystery."[95]

Another contemporary writer quick to affirm what happens in preaching is Paul Scott Wilson, whose first chapter in his latest writing speaks without equivocation: "We claim that preaching is an event in which the congregation meets the living God."[96] Or again: "God uses the sermon for self-revelation, for it is in the reading and correct interpretation of Scripture (a safeguard provided by our traditions) that God chooses most to be revealed."[97] Not that God *might* choose or *sometimes* choose, but "chooses most." And what might it mean to speak of a "correct interpretation" (singular form) that is a safeguard provided by "traditions" (plural form)?

Regarding Buttrick and Wilson, each seems to be certain on different sides of a triangular equation (involving God/preacher/congregation). Wilson's certitude seems to operate between God and the preacher (an understanding about revelation); Buttrick's certitude operates between the preacher and the people (an understanding about communication and consciousness).

Actually, Lucy Rose is also certain—but with a much different and more modest homiletical purpose. Since in her view of conversational preaching, the preacher is not intending primarily to "win consent . . . to a truth claim," we need not worry whether such a thing might happen. Since the preacher does not expect a radical divine in-breaking or a transforming event, these issues are not key to the question of being certain.[98]

"Does preaching's content slide into the quagmire of relativism where everything is slippery and unstable?" she asks. Her answer: "No. In conversational preaching the sermon's content is a proposal offered to the community of faith . . . a wager on the part of the preacher."[99] To make an offer is the goal. It would be difficult to ever suggest it didn't happen.

At the other extreme is Dietrich Ritschl, who in his work *A Theology of Proclamation*, declared that "the Word, which is Jesus

Christ, shall perform its own work. Therefore it must be said that the sermon will not only create individually life and faith, but it will also determine the history of the world."[100] Now, *that* is certainty.

We should notice that those who are certain about the goals of preaching happening in the sermonic event are drawn from all our homiletical categories. Their sense of homiletical purpose may be different from another, but the certainty they hold in common.

On the Other Hand

But then again, there are some who are not at all so sure that what we *hope* will happen in fact *does* happen come Sunday. Some might wonder what it could possibly mean never to be disappointed on Sunday afternoon—or for that matter, to be flooded with joy not of one's own making. What is the connection between our plans and what may or not happen?

Barbara Brown Taylor notes, for example, that "something happens between the preacher's lips and the congregation's ears that is beyond prediction or explanation." Not only is it the case that "the same sermon sounds entirely different at 9:00 and 11:15 A.M. on a Sunday morning," it is that "later in the week, someone quotes part of my sermon back to me . . . only I never said it. There is more going on here than anyone can say."[101]

Yes, indeed, there is something going on, sometimes for good and sometimes not. Note the tentativeness between *intention* and *result* captured in Craddock's description. In the very last paragraph of his chapter "A Theology of Preaching," he speaks what he says should always be the "final word" in any such discussion: "A theology of preaching is an acknowledgment of its provisional nature."

Such a theology must presume the right for the preacher to grow and mature and also make no claim or demand upon God in the process.

A theology of preaching is no more than an attempt to discern the way of God's Word in the world and to align one's mode and matter of preaching accordingly. The minister never says, "This is the way

God will work through preaching," but rather he or she says, "This is the way I work because of my understanding of the way God works." But even then, surprises wait at every corner.[102]

Sometimes the surprise is magnificent—as described by James Cone: "The Word is more than *words* about God. God's Word is a poetic happening, an evocation of an indescribable reality in the lives of the people."[103] Sometimes the surprise is otherwise. Rebecca Chopp explains that "the relation between Word and words is one of meaning, presence, and signification, but also one of gaps, inexpressibility, rupture, and chaos."[104]

But note Cone's central term *evocation*. The term serves us well here in trying to discern what does or does not happen in the sermon. That's the term David Randolph used more than two decades ago: "Preaching is understood not as the packaging of a product but as the evocation of an event."[105]

The term *evocation* reminds me of a text I once had to study in a graduate school of education. The text was *The Activities of Teaching*, by Thomas F. Green, in which he drew from the work of Gilbert Ryle relative to category mistakes—namely, the difference between *task* and *achievement* terms, which sometimes appear to involve causality and yet sometimes exert their independence.[106]

He explains how the task-achievement pair of *looking* and *finding* are related—namely, that looking sometimes prompts finding, but then again, sometimes finding has nothing whatever to do with looking. Noting that *teaching* and *learning* represent another pair of task-achievement terms, he asks whether teaching could be going on if no learning was happening. It seemed like a foolish question to me—obviously to be answered in the negative. It is, however, analogous to the question of whether there can be *preaching* going on if no one is experiencing the Word. And I can assure you that in this case the answer is, unfortunately, yes; it does often happen. Sometimes I have been the preacher.

Green explains the difference between task and achievement terms. For example, one can go fishing and never catch anything. *Fishing* is a task term. On the other hand, can a person go swimming without getting wet in the pool? No, because *swimming* is an achievement term.

By analogy I want to assert that *preaching* is a task term. It is what we do. Said one knowledgeable in such things: "In making a sermon the preacher makes something" the preacher "cannot control and whose future" the preacher "cannot predict."[107] Good preachers, says David Schlafer, "choose strategies that evoke rather than exhort, and offer rather than order."[108]

There is that word again: *evoke!* Preaching is an *offering* intending to evoke an event that cannot be coerced into being. "The trick in preaching," Buttrick says, "is to use an ordinary vocabulary in the extraordinary service of the gospel, dancing the edge of mystery."[109] Yes, that is it. Buttrick's term for it is *invocation.*[110]

Well, if *preaching* is a task term—to use Green's formula—what is the corresponding achievement term? The achievement term I choose is *proclaiming.* Proclaiming the Word.

Preaching I can do. I choose it; I prepare for it. Prayerfully I engage it, and I perform it. I do it. I will do it Sunday next. Proclaiming the Word is what I *hope* will happen next Sunday. I will attempt my preparation strategy in such a way as to maximize the chance for it. But proclaiming the Word? Nobody has the grip of control for it. You cannot capture it; you cannot possess it; you cannot package it; you cannot deliver it, and you cannot control the receipt of it. Sorry. Preaching the sermon is a *task;* proclaiming the Word is the hoped-for *goal.* It would be an achievement indeed.

The bridge between sermonic task and achievement, the bridge between preaching and proclaiming is *evocation.*

Back in 1958, when H. Grady Davis's powerful work on preaching emerged, there was another homiletical book of historic dimensions: *The Ministry of the Word,* by R. E. C. Browne—an English cleric and poet. (He just now reminded us that the preacher cannot control or even predict the result of sermons.)

So profound is the book's content that when Craddock's textbook *Preaching* came to its final page, another page was added for "Suggested Resources." The first such resource named was the book by Browne. Declared Craddock: "It bears rereading every three to four years."

"Ultimately the preacher's work," says Browne, "is to help people to be in a state of mind where perception is possible, that is, in a state where their minds are open and receptive to the divine action."[111] Such a view is sobering to preachers who have difficulty discerning the difference between human words and the divine Word. The bottom line for Browne is the startling idea that "in a sense the sermon does not matter, what matters is what the preacher cannot say because the ineffable remains the ineffable and all that can be done is to make gestures towards it with the finest words that can be used."[112] No wonder Browne had no use for single-sentence summaries of sermons: "If all that a sermon . . . said could be put in one sentence, would there be any point in making sermons?"[113] Yet, "from time to time," he observes, "blunt sentences will reverberate with the ineffable" and "lips will proclaim things" the preacher cannot know.[114]

Sometimes. From time to time.

Preaching is our task. Proclaiming the Word is the realized goal. Perhaps the act of evocation may become the bridge, the spanning medium of possibility between preaching and proclaiming.

3

ACT · ART

I find the phrase "act of evocation" particularly helpful and useful—at least—at one level. But when Browne's claim is taken seriously, that "the ineffable remains the ineffable," the phrase "act of evocation" no longer feels so self-evident. What, precisely, are we evoking? If theologian Hendrikus Berkhof is correct that the *first* thing that God reveals is God's hiddenness—that God "does not by that act cease to be the hidden God"[115]—I want to know what the *second* thing is. What is left to be revealed?

Feminist theologian Rebecca Chopp acknowledges that one view—not her own—perceives "an unabridgeable gap between God and world." If this view is correct, any hope for evocation is, of course, dead. Not so, she argues: "My understanding of proclamation . . . argues for a relationship between gap and connection." She continues, "Language itself, after all, depends upon a certain intersubjectivity, an interconnectedness that bridges gaps—else why would we need speech? Yet language is utterly dependent upon the gap, abyss, and separation that require communication."[116]

Interconnectedness. That will be our presumption here. One critical question, then, will be: *What kind of language best says what cannot be spoken and gives what cannot be possessed?* Understand, this will not be the only kind of question, because of our wide concern in this chapter for the content of preaching. But it will be our opening question.

Meanwhile, interconnectedness cannot be set into some sort of assumed pipeline connection ("just me and Jesus" thinking). The moment one uses the term *language* we are set in a social context. Surely, the title of Peter Berger and Thomas Luckmann's book *The Social Construction of Reality* of decades past says it all.

The Social Context of Our Preaching

Although in North America many of us have learned to presume otherwise, we simply cannot talk about the sermon or any kind of meaning outside the communal context. P. T. Forsyth put the matter boldly: "The one great preacher in history, I would contend, is the Church."[117] The individual preacher is called "to preach to the Church," but also must "preach *from* the Church."[118] From another perspective: "Every sermon," maintains Arthur Van Seters, "is uttered by *socialized* beings to a *social* entity in a specific *social* context and always at a *social* moment."[119] More philosophically viewed: "It is not as though . . . [a person] begins as a purely individual consciousness . . . and then casts about for . . . some higher significance," says Stephen Crites. "People awaken to consciousness in a society . . . already infused with cultural forms."[120] Concludes Van Seters: "All preaching then is a social act."[121]

Whatever one does with the question of public theology—that is, of the possibility of speaking outside the parameters of social location (and there is more than one credible view here)—language is not just "learned"; it is given. It is a principal reason why, as someone once put it, we are all born with a history—a history mediated by language.

We need to understand not only the "communal character of language and the linguistic constitution of community," Chopp notes, but also the impact of "communicative solidarity with human words, relations, and actions."[122]

Browne identifies a central issue that lies underneath our current concern about sermonic language—indeed notes a confusion regarding homiletical communication. "What a person believes about the mode of divine revelation should determine the mode of . . . [one's] preaching," he observes. Preachers who believe that divine revelation is given in propositional form will, of course, develop sermons that correspond to that view. Inspiration would consist of "being given the right propositions" for use in the preaching occasion. Those who don't, won't. Except, he explains, many who don't, still do.

> Many who deny the literal inspiration of the Scriptures govern their work as preachers by doctrinal principles which assume that divine revelation is given in proposition. The form of their sermons denies implicitly what they state explicitly about the mode of revelation.[123]

Notice the implications here. If you are a biblical literalist, likely you will not be greatly interested in homiletical acts of evocation. You will simply repeat what you believe God said—and that's the end of the matter. Mystery no more; it is swallowed up by absolute knowledge. It is all very consistent.

But if you lean toward another view—such as that held by H. Grady Davis who said, "The truth we preach is not an abstract thing. The truth is a Person"[124]—well then language use may have to turn to analogy and even metaphor to satisfy the consequences of your view.

Or again, your evangelistic sermon conclusion leads you to choose the closing gospel hymn with that rousing chorus line: "And he walks with me and he talks with me," and you later reflect that it was no ordinary walk. The garden was in the Holy Land then and the walk happened here today—and the voice was a bit different from the neighbor next door. The gospel song's lyrics lean away from normal speech by analogy. The lyrics are an attempt at evocative language making extraordinary claims. (By the way, we should note the privatistic assumption also quietly undergirded by that song.) The first step toward the sermonic act of evocation is to notice how commonplace such language use is, particularly in liturgical acts.

My observation is that in the last decade of increased mainline Protestant use of the common lectionary, sermons—on average—have become more biblical, more boring, and less evocative. The postsermon phrase "I think I got it across" is a telling remark, suggesting that the sermon had leaned heavily toward discursive instruction and with only light or absent evocation.

Part of this phenomenon that I am claiming may be due to the all-too-quick utilization of expert commentaries prior to the lection getting hold of the preacher. Often, I am afraid, it may have to do with the selection process of the lectionary committee—whose choices tend toward either doxological affirmations or longer explanations in didactic form.

Whatever the case, it is too easy to leave the dance at the edge of mystery and to plod along the road of truth (not a capital *t*). Could this be the mind-set of modernity at its worst? Certainly, it reflects the exegetical methodology many of us were taught to engage. Gene Tucker suggests that "historical-critical inquiry draws attention away from the text and to its context." Often the mentality leans toward "disinterested inquiry," sometimes moving toward the "single 'correct' meaning to be abstracted" from the passage. Instead, Tucker urges greater intentionality be focused upon the "world created by the reading of the text."[125]

Most varieties of biblical narrative criticism—including, for example, both the pure narrativist view of Frei and the revisionist view of Riceour—nonetheless share the common intentionality to assist us in exploring the multidimensions of biblical story that cannot so quickly be translated into settled doctrinal points.

There are exceptions, of course. One writer in narrative theology and preaching, Mark Ellingsen, has a quite different agenda. His stated reasons for throwing out any determination of a text's situation-in-life is that biblical/historical scholarship can never be absolutely certain. The "results of historical research are only probable, always open to revision. . . . That the Word of God may be uncertain is not a tolerable situation for Christian theology."[126] To which I say, welcome to the human community.

Moreover, he believes "at least in principle" that critical literary analysis can provide the basis for "certainties, rather than probabilities."[127] How Ellingsen hopes to avoid the indeterminancies of human point of view in literary analysis is unclear to me. The lack of absolute certainty may seem intolerable to him; I call it inevitable. Inevitable and preferable. "Is there a poet," asks Brueggemann "who can render the text clearly without fuzziness, but also without a seducing certitude that covers over where I live?"[128]

Writing back in the late 1950s, Browne noted that "modern scientists do not claim to be able to give a literal description of the universe." Indeed, "they say that the most accurate measuring and weighing are no more than . . . approximations." Little wonder, then, that poets admit they "never mean exactly what they say because they cannot say exactly what they mean."[129]

> If the Gospel were a set of propositions then the language of apologetics, in and out of the pulpit, would depend on a mastery of prose, but if the centre of the Gospel is a person then the language of Christianity must have a marked dependence on poetry.[130]

Does this mean, then, that our homiletical concern for the act of evocation suggests we dispense with discursive thought? After all, Sallie McFague has assisted us in understanding that "doctrine is the sedimentation of metaphors" and "the agreed-upon understanding of . . . images."[131] So, such doctrine represents language that is "older," further removed from the original metaphoric beginning.

In this context, we can surely agree that such doctrinally shaped views are in form less homiletically evocative—whereas analogy, metaphoric tease, and the tensiveness of parabolic thought provide great potential for the evocation we are seeking.

But before we jump into some kind of doctrineless, positionless abyss, we need to hear Browne once more—who may surprise us with his conviction that "belief in preaching, or indeed in meaningful conversation, has doctrinal roots or else it has no roots."[132]

We ought to notice that the metaphoric tease has no tease at all without the discursive pole. If one defines a metaphor as a figure of speech that tensively teases meaning by bringing together two apparently dissimilar perceptual realities, one known and the other not, then without the "known" the metaphoric moment cannot happen.

"What poets do," says McFague, "is to take our literal words, our dead metaphors, and by combining them in new ways, make them capable of expressing new insight."[133] Or again, she says that the new insight comes "by framing the ordinary in an extraordinary context."[134] No wonder Gabrielle Rico calls metaphor the "bilinguist" of the brain.

Is it not the case that metaphoric thinking (to shape a metaphor here) is a kind of *peripheral vision?* Sometimes the best way to look at something is to catch a glimpse out of the corner of your eye. Sometimes it is the only way. (Surely, Moses understood. Once, you recall, the Lord covered Moses' face until the Lord had completely passed by. All that was left for Moses to see was a glimpse out of the corner of the eye.) Speaking in the context of sacramental speech, Brueggemann appropriately warns the preacher to avoid "direct, frontal speech."[135]

And why should we be concerned for such things? Because the rather large question looming just now—particularly in the context of postmodern thought—is the question of the *content* of our preaching. Hence, the issue of language modes and of their interdependence becomes central to us at this moment in time.

Browne's description of how ministers in his time were torn between two equally unacceptable views is remarkably contemporary with current conversations: "Thus, the minister of the Word is dealing on the one hand with old-fashioned rationalists and on the other hand with irrationalists or potential irrationalists." The preacher is caught trying to "safeguard the validity of reason without encouraging rationalists to fancy that he is denying the reality of mental processes other than discursive reasoning." That's half of it. The other half is the preacher's concern to not lend support "to the irrationalist's notion that discursive reasoning is obsolete."[136]

Translated to our day and our concerns for the sermon, in my view it means trying to get unhooked from modernity's commitment to unchanging "stared at" discursive truth on the one hand, and yet managing to not succumb to the ghetto-of-one mentality of the skeptical postmodernists on the other.

The Problem of Staring at the Truth

Every pastor knows what it is like on a Sunday afternoon to reflect happily on the morning message. For once "it got said"

and in a way people understood. The preacher had been compli-
mented for clarity. Then in a moment of fond recollection, the
pastor remembers the sermon preached only a few weeks back—
and recalls that the "message" of that day was the reverse of
today's word. Immediately, the preacher hopes enough time has
elapsed for folks to have forgotten. (The preacher need not
worry.) I have known pastors even to retrieve notes of the previous sermon to check how bad the contradiction. I know; I have
done it.

But it was a different text and a different moment in the life of
the congregation. What was said then may have been as true for
that occasion as this truth is for today. Pastors with more than one
congregation in the parish know how a sermon's message sometimes gets altered in the car between services, because the two
congregations are so different that the "word from the Lord" from
the same text will have to be different.

Propositional truth delivered through discursive language has
a way of sounding more eternally true than it really is, even after
we have researched the matter. Somehow the mystery loses its
awe and the preacher loses the edge where dancing happens.
"The speech of poetry," notes Brueggemann, will "keep hidden
what must not be profaned by description."[137]

I once declared propositional truth to be the corpse of what was
once lived experience. Even though I added how important it is
for physicians-in-training to work with cadavers for the sake of
our health, some responders could not hear the caveat. There
must be some way to hold a proper suspicion of the ways we
name things without having to discard our best reflective thinking. Our language, too, participates in our peculiar slant in view-
ing truth. Somewhere, Benjamin Whorf once said that we think
what we can *say* is dependent upon what we can *see;* actually,
what we can *see* is dependent upon what we can *say.*

The writer most helpful for me at this point is Robert Roth who,
in concern for "the vitality of the original stories," notes the
natural sequence of a religious community's life: "First came the
religious vision, then the aesthetic expression of it, then the ethical
emulation of it, and finally the philosophical rationalization as

explanation and apology." But he concludes: "My contention is that the story itself is reality."[138]

The vision is this reality—borne by the story. I hope he didn't mean that the other three levels are false. I would want to insist that in the collective wisdom of the ongoing history of the church's tradition, all four levels relate in an interdependent way—and all bear the mark "true." All four are real. Clearly, the mode of reality is different—*how* they are true shifts focus and observability. Yet at different levels all four are real. At the same time I understand and concur in his commitment to highlight what he believes to be central.

Nonetheless, if the vision cannot survive being tested by the hardest questions of the best logic of the time—as well as live with the most fitting discursive definition available—then the vision will either turn foolish and be rejected or simply evaporate out of the community's memory. There should be a sweep back and forth, from vision through aesthetic and ethical levels to rational explanation—and then back again—repeatedly. This is how the community checks the vision; this is how the community tests the philosophical rationality.

Yet, a scholastic spirit often takes the most creative theological constructions of the previous generation—forged often in the fires of vulnerability—and will then encase that truth in concrete and set it up as a shrine. End of discussion.

For example, Jesus dies on the cross and Paul uses four images in a span of two verses for understanding the meaning of his death. By and by these metaphoric images become doctrines, and then become litmus test material for checking doctrinal purity. If you do not accept, for example, the substitutionary theory of the Atonement, you will not be able to use your scholarly skills around certain biblical tables. It all started out as a metaphor.

Right now the church is arguing about God language, and this process can be observed firsthand. We have been through it before for centuries. Well, not the same issue, but the same process, which generally winds up with at least two sets of concluding charges: heresy and/or idolatry. The truth is (so to speak) that the dangers for false witness, inadequate formulation, and imbalanced emphasis are always close by. Browne says, "To think positively is to discover that the minister of the Word's true doctrinal position is always on the fringes of error."[139]

Particularly when dealing with the "ineffable," the church is called toward the *eloquence of the provisional.* Such speech declares the truth, all the while knowing the truth cannot be uttered. The travelers on the Emmaus road found that out. After they instructed the stranger about the truth, the real truth got revealed in the breaking of bread, and—wouldn't you know it—the moment they thought they were going to get their hands on it, the presence of the truth disappeared. They were left with only a glimpse in the corner of their eyes. But its power turned them around nonetheless.

In matters theological it is unbecoming for us to stare at the truth eyeball to eyeball. Evocation never works that way.

And What Is Truth?

Pilate was not the last to ask. It seems that we are asking his question in quite new ways in the past couple decades—or is it more accurate to suggest that others have been asking for a couple decades and the rest of us are just beginning to notice the question? All of which, by the way, comes with great shock to many folks in our generation.

Many of us have been wonderfully innocent of our own modernity. It has come so easily, so conveniently. Simply, we have presumed the rationality of the species in terms fitting our own sense of being human and have likely presumed the universality of human experience in ways compatible with the world we know. Of course we have. But a few things have been happening while we were not looking.

As a mainline Protestant preacher in preparation, I was taught in seminary to utilize the tools of modern historical-critical analysis. I never heard such terms as *postmodern, social location,* and *incommensurability.* I was taught to ask the proper higher-critical questions. My blue copy of *Gospel Parallels* was never far away. Whatever the synoptic text, I reviewed again the question of synoptic formation with Mark coming first, not Matthew, and noted how differently Luke understood the disciples' miscues (seems that they were always "kept" from the truth). Different settings, different purposes, different ways of speaking—all these are important before you can assess what the passage "wants to say"—by which was meant the "correct message." Sometimes I learned a lot *about* a text.

Strangely, it was often the case that the longer I did my homework for a passage, the farther from the sermon I became. Indeed, through the years I have had more than a few preachers confide that they had learned through the years to not engage in too much exegetical work; it just seemed to shut sermonic doors.

In retrospect—and with the help of biblical experts—it appears that our work seemed always to be taking things apart. And that the bottom-line truth, message, or point for the sermon often seemed to be found not in the text at all, but underneath it or behind it. The text became an objective thing to be dissected—as though looking *through* it to some truth more basic or universal.

Biblical work was and is always so much more than this description suggests. But this description reveals a tendency or leaning that exposes itself particularly when the work toward Sunday is not going well. My experience with biblical narrative criticism has been liberating (well, some of it has). Narrative biblical work intends to keep the spotlight of attention on the text itself. This approach seems more interested in the unity of a passage than in its divisive past. For this preacher, at least, such a biblical approach has most often been very user-friendly.

Not that narrative criticism has no dangers, of course. Preachers employing narrative biblical criticism can walk the road of eisegesis as well and as quickly as anybody else—maybe more quickly if one thinks that a text's meaning is actually self-referential and self-evident (with the preacher being the "self").

Moreover—in my view—the "world created by the reading of the text,"[140] as Tucker describes it, needs more attention than simply being "passively privileged." For example, Frei and Ricoeur "agree on many things," notes Gary Comstock, but as to whether a particular biblical narrative is true, they disagree. Both find such narratives essential, but "only Ricoeur believes that we can or should try to justify this belief as true."[141]

Particularly helpful to preachers, I believe, is Mark Allan Powell's *What Is Narrative Criticism?* It takes the readers by the hand gently and convincingly through really important questions. For example, Powell, as a narrativist, deals with the question of the relationship of literary and historical inquiry. Using the metaphors of *window* and *mirror*, Powell says literary critics do not

> question the legitimacy of historical inquiry. It should not be assumed that they naively accept whatever they read as perfectly historical or that they view the Bible as a collection of tales with little basis in reality. Rather, these critics bracket out questions of historicity in order to concentrate on the nature of the text as literature. They do not deny that biblical narratives may also serve a referential function or that it may be rewarding to study them in that regard as well.[142]

David L. Bartlett powerfully names an important corrective to potential excesses with certain forms of narrative criticism when he reminds preachers that "we cannot be faithful to the text as literature without attending to the history behind the text." Moreover: "If we simply use the text as a Rorschach blot for our own theological intuitions, of course, that's another matter; but that is not what most advocates of literary criticism or narrative preaching are advocating."[143]

Beyond the issue of the forms of biblical scholarship is the question of truth itself. Some postmodernist writers of the radical or skeptical variety insist that no one has any right to make any kind of truth claim—that, in fact, there are no universal truths. (Would such a statement constitute one?) William C. Placher in *Unapologetic Theology* describes the prominent view of Hans Frei "who proposes a radical solution." Regarding questions that concern the truthfulness of biblical narratives, either the question of historicity or of general moral lessons, Placher summarizes Frei's view in this way:

> Suppose we do not start with the modern world. Suppose we start with the biblical world, and let those narratives define what is real, so that *our* lives have meaning to the extent that we fit them into *that* framework. . . . If we do that, then the truth of the biblical narratives does not depend on connecting them to some other *real* world. *They* describe the real world.[144]

Well, that is not sufficient for some. Paul Ricoeur, seen as the other chief participant in early conversations on this matter, has further concerns. For Ricoeur, "religious utterances do make publicly intelligible claims about what is the case, and they do refer."[145] As a result, listeners and/or readers have to decide whether to say "yes" or "no" to the claims made. Ricoeur wants to know what grounds anybody has to make such a decision. ·

Stanley Hauerwas finds altogether different grounds for assessing truth claims of religious narratives—namely, looking at the results they cause. He states, "Just as scientific theories are partially judged by the fruitfulness of the activities they generate, so narratives can and should be judged by the richness of moral character and activity they generate."[146] Or as he put it on another occasion with coauthor David Burrell: "The test of each story is the sort of person it shapes."[147]

But this explanation does not satisfy Placher: "We do something because God did something first. Therefore, it cannot be the virtue of our people or the practices of our community that make true the story we tell about what God did."[148]

Sometimes it is difficult to know precisely what is meant by what an author is saying in this regard, and in this time of transition many of us are having to wait a while before jumping in with a response. For example, Thomas H. Troeger discusses the connection between poetics and homiletics, as he understands it. So he wants the reader to understand that he is using the term *poetics* in the sense of "the character of our articulation of reality as it arises from our historically conditioned imaginative construction of the world."[149]

Well, many will want to know what direction he means to take by this statement. Is his focus on *imagination* and, hence, is being modest rather than dogmatic by acknowledging his historical contingency, or is his focus on *construction*, suggesting that poetics is utterly self-referential only? It makes a world of difference. Certainly, agreement comes easily regarding his belief that the church must "find some way of proclaiming a redeeming vision for humanity without the absolutism of universal dogmatic assurance."[150] We just need to know what lies behind that conclusion—in short, what route he hopes we will travel together to this destination of thought.

While writers may seem to be saying the same thing, there is a vast difference of reluctance between the mystical poet and the skeptical postmodernist. Sometimes it is the difference between cynicism and humility. My hunch is that hymn writer Troeger opts for the focus on imagination's humility.

The bottom line for Placher regarding possible answers to the question of "what is truth?" is to find a middle ground between "two challenges, one from either side." He continues:

> One side would claim that the Enlightenment was right, and we really do have to find universally acceptable common ground for rational conversations. The other side would insist that we cannot find such common ground and as a result people from different traditions cannot talk to one another at all.[151]

Is this formulation of the issue by Placher not remarkably similar to that posed by R. E. C. Browne in 1958, about the polarities of two unacceptable positions, offered by the rationalists and the irrationalists? We might notice, also, a remarkably familiar ring between Browne's repeated statement of comparative similarities of preaching and poetry to Ricoeur's conclusion that the "truth claims of religious texts are more like those of the poet than of the historian or the scientist."[152]

The "bottom line" for Placher (and for this writing as well) is that "to the extent that I take the pattern of these stories to be the pattern for my life and of the world, I am committed to believing that the God they describe is not the projection or useful construct of the people in the story." Moreover, says Placher, "to the extent that the pattern these stories provide me becomes compelling in the way that a pattern can, then I will acknowledge their claims about God, however still mysterious."[153]

The consequence of such a view is to believe that, however sketchy or lacking in final absolutist claims, nonetheless the Christian vision has "got hold of something fundamentally right about the overall picture" and that "someday" confirmation for all will emerge. It is interesting that Placher speaks of such a moment of sensing a pattern as when we "catch a glimpse."[154]

In the earlier discussion of Craddock's views on the theology of preaching, we heard him say that "a theology of preaching is no more than an attempt to discern the way of God's Word in the world and to align one's mode and matter of preaching accordingly."[155] Notice how strikingly compatible the term *align* is to this current discussion.

So Craddock wants the preacher to *align* the sermon toward the way of God's Word, Placher advises us to sense the divine *pattern*, Browne hopes we will *gesture* toward the ineffable, Buttrick invites us to *dance* the edge of mystery, and I trust we will do our best to *evoke* the proclamation. All of these points of view signal a commonly felt consequence—seems to me. In our best homiletical labor, it is as though we are so close to the heart of some matter that we might just reach out and touch it. It is as though we are dancing the edge of mystery. Of course, if we could and did actually touch it, then it obviously would *not* be that moment of revelation for which we had hoped. But sometimes one can feel it coming ever so close by. Given such proximity, we dare to move toward the *eloquence of the provisional*, which may be less than we think we want, but certainly is more than we might have reason to expect.

Not long ago I was visiting with Jud Souers, a close friend who pastors in Phoenix. In conversation about the sermon event, he said, "I see myself as a stagehand who holds back the curtain so that some might be able to catch a glimpse of the divine play—sometimes—perhaps—if I can get it open enough."

That's how close. If we could just get a better handle on how to pull back the curtain.

From Stagehand to Midwife

The power of Souers' metaphor of preacher as stagehand comes in the evocational sensibility it produces—of giftedness of proximity, of faithful confidence about life on stage, and of community presence.

The preacher is not inventing stuff or even introducing something. Nor does the preacher facilitate a world in front of a text known only by the contemporary company it keeps. The preacher facilitates a glimpse into what the Christian community believes God is doing in the world. Is this not what Placher means by sensing a pattern? Little wonder Davis chose the organic metaphor of tree, not some mechanical analogy for the sermon.

The basic sermonic idea—that is "born somehow,"[156] says Davis—"must have in it a force that is expanding."[157] He calls it the "generative idea."[158] Again, note the deeply held assumption. Like a tree, life is going on. The sermon names and claims again that life. All of which is to say that indirection is often a key component to the preparation process—together with prayerful patience.

Taylor talks about how she waits:

> This is the gestation period of a sermon, and it cannot be rushed. It is a time of patient and impatient waiting for the stirring of the Holy Spirit, that bright bird upon whose brooding the sermon depends. Over and over again I check the nest of my notes and outlines, searching . . . for some sign of life. I scan the text one more time and all of a sudden there is an egg in plain view, something where there had been nothing just a moment before, and the sermon is born.[159]

"The poet," says Eliseo Vivas, aesthetic epistemologist, "is a midwife and uses the forceps of language."[160] That imagery is a particularly helpful correction for those of us busily going around making points. Rather, life is being born, and the effective preacher as midwife knows when to be still so as not to impede the birthing process—and when to be feverishly active in preventing some blockage from denying the life that wants to be.

"Moved by forces over which . . . [one] exercises only limited conscious control," says Vivas, "the artist . . . does not know clearly what he [sic] wants to say till the labor of the file is finished." Then the artist "can discover" the "intentions" in the composition.[161]

4

SHAPE ·· STRATEGY

*H*ow, then, might we define the sermon shapes that are consistent or compatible with the sermon as described here? The answer depends on what factor of sermonic form is central to the evocation we intend. In broadest terms—and given a multitude of theoretically descriptive forms—*movement* is central. We have already mentioned the issue briefly in noting several contemporary options for preaching. Now we need to press the matter further.

We all know when movement happens for us—no matter how we were taught to shape the sermon. During our preparation for Sunday, it sometimes happens that we get pushed out of the driver's seat of our own work and get taken for a ride. The heartbeat tells us about it in no uncertain terms. Surely, it has something to do with H. Grady Davis' insistence that a sermonic idea has an expanding force—apparently a life of its own—and we get swept along.

I have often noticed that the sermons that seem to "fly" as some might describe it, and ones that "crash" as many of us all too often experience it, turn somehow around a single factor that can be observed in the preparation process—and hence guessed in advance. When in our preparation we continue to look for things to add to the sermon—an extra illustration here and another supplemental text there—likely, the sermon is in trouble come Sunday. In fact, the sermon probably does not need the additional illustration or other text for that matter; probably, it needs some kind of internal expansive force. Without accurately naming the need, however, we hope the addition of another piece will get it going. It seldom does.

On the other hand, when the preparation procedure involves deletion, trimming, and pruning, likely, good things are in store when Sunday comes. Such a sermon, as Robin Meyers describes it, is not so much "worked up" as it is "worked out."[162] Again, interior energy is present, and wisely, we know how to remove factors that are in the way.

The centrality of movement. You can feel it inside Craddock's observation that preaching depends not just in getting something said but in getting it heard. Paul Scott Wilson named it well when he said, "We want something that will encourage us to think of the sermon . . . as growing, organic, or living, as having movement and rhythm." Hence, we may choose to "talk about the flow."[163] To do so is not simply to be "fiddling with sermon form."[164] Such issues as order, arrangement, and pattern, says M. Eugene Boring, "help the sermon to flow" toward the desired goal of "bearing the hearers along with its movement."[165] This is but one reason why "the form of a sermon," as Tom Long confirms, "is itself a theological issue."[166] At its deepest level, sermonic movement has to do with working with some kind of life force, which just may issue in a live birth.

As we noted earlier, basic to sermon movement—whether of ideas, action, images, or story—is a principle regarding *sequence*. "Change the order of the phrases and ideas," notes Craddock, "and you have a quite different message."[167] And sequence is seldom natural or innocent. Sequence is strategic.

One could speak of the basic *musicality* of any sermon. Music, after all, is also an event-in-time art form, with melody, harmony, and rhythm coming sequentially. No one *builds* a song; it is shaped and performed. In the classroom I like to move to a piano and announce to the class that I am about to play the melody notes of a favorite hymn. With one finger of my right hand I play the following:

CCCCCCDDDFFFFFFFFFFFGGGAAAAAAAAACCC

After feigning shock that no one could name this well-known hymn, I announce it to have been "Amazing Grace." "Well," I admit, "I didn't play the notes *in sequence.*" Without proper sequence it is in fact *not* "Amazing Grace." A joke beginning with the "punch line" is not a joke; the story of Noah building the ark beginning with a completed ship is not a story of Noah building the ark. Content and form are inseparable. There is no such thing as formless content. We may have poorly formed thought, but never no-formed thought.

When the subject at hand is evocative preaching that might just dance the edge of inarticulatable mystery, this point cannot be overstated. One cannot garner some ideas *and then* see how to serve them; one finds their potential placement in the *interior energy* of the temporal sequence called the sermon. "The rationalist notion that we have preformed thought," observes Buttrick, "which we can put into word containers for shipment to someone else's mind is simply not true."[168]

And what makes for "interior energy"? What did Meyers mean in speaking of a sermon "working itself out"? On what basis might a preacher get "swept along" in the preparation process? What "trip" is meant that cannot be "totally anticipated"? What "flow" do I have in mind? And to what temporal sequence strategy do I refer? The answer, of course, is plot.

The Plot

It is possible that the term *plot* for some people may denote a quite narrow band of meaning. Perhaps Aristotle's description of a classic tragedy comes to mind or, for others, that favorite television sitcom. For the sake of expanding our thinking here, why not consider shopping at the supermarket?

A good grocery list, you understand, will be properly plotted. That is, such a list ought not be simply a grocery list of needed items—as the stereotype goes—but a temporal sequence, stragegically shaped. Effective shopping is made possible when the list assists us to move not simply from *this* to *that*, but from *here* to *there*. The store's placement of entry, the front door, to its cash register exits—and every aisle in between—contributes to the shaping of the plot. And the items listed for purchase will fall into place as we move through the aisles with dispatch. No need to waste time and energy by retracing one's steps. The shopping plot will unfold properly—with a startling and decisive monetary reversal, followed by the final restful denouement couched in the closing question: "Paper or plastic?"

Likewise, every plotting operation must be considered in its context, which involves multiple layers of other plotted realities—coming and going. To continue our illustration: Once inside the kitchen, the one plot empties into another that thickens—on the stove—which then later participates in an ever-more complicated plot involving the arrival of the newly assigned supervisor as guest for dinner. When the host gives thanks for the food, everybody (perhaps) gets involved in a plot of ontic dimensions.

Frank Kermode once had the audacity to consider the matter of plot as paradigmatically modeled by the tick and tock of an ordinary clock. Notice, he said, both the "humble genesis" of tick and the "feeble apocalypse of tock." Following every tick is "organized duration"; following every tock is an "unorganized blank."[169] Can you remember ever attempting by sheer determination of the will to reverse the two sounds of tick and tock? They *were* two different sounds, weren't they?

And again, sometimes our most crucial plotting attempts have come not in the sermon but in the strategy of church administration, as we work diligently in attempting to negotiate a critical resolution through the minefield labyrinth of institutional bureaucracy. The important of sequence, the nuance of timing, the happenstance of exterior events. Plotting the meeting is not easy.

The point of these quick images of music, grocery stores, clocks, and institutional life is to reaffirm the need to position the term *plot* in settings both particular and diverse. Even when our field of interest constricts the subject to oral presentation in general and the sermon in particular, the subject of plot is a multifaceted reality. Whatever the diversity of types of contemporary new homiletic preaching, all involve a *sequencing strategy* "in which the arrangement of ideas takes the form of a plot involving a strategic delay of the preacher's meaning."[170]

The above citation is taken from a section I wrote for the *Concise Encyclopedia of Preaching*. Those who are familiar with my previous writings will not be surprised to know that the encyclopedia section in question was titled "narrative preaching." The above statement was my definition of a narrative sermon. Hence the natural question now: If finally we have come around to the constant theme of all my writings—namely, advocacy for narrative preaching—why did I not say so before now? Why not be up front about it?

Actually, both editorial staff and I originally planned to utilize the term *narrative* as the overall focus for this writing. Indeed, in *Listening to the Word*,[171] I utilized the term *narrative* as the umbrella designation for all six types of preaching described here—and can still defend that choice. Two considerations prompt the present focus on plot.

First, there is still confusion regarding the terms *narrative* and *story*. Many still seem not to understand that the term *narrative* can refer either to the temporal sequencing of the sermonic source (narrative text) or to the narrative sequencing of the presentation (narrative oral discourse)—or to both. Following this wonderfully clear definition by Craven means, for example, that a plotted sermon on the "prodigal son story" is a *narrative*, narrative sermon—that is, it involves both narrative *source* and narrative *treatment*. Be that as it may, some simply presume that the term *narrative* equals story. (Thus, many of us interested in narrative preaching often are inaccurately listed as "story preachers.")

Second, others seem to presume that all "narrative sermons" involve the same homiletical sequence without variation. Such a reductionist view is like saying all the parables of Jesus are the same: when you have met one, you have met them all. This, of course, would be equivalent to presuming that all traditionally shaped sermons look and hear alike. I hope that the discussion thus far in this chapter will help to dispel that idea (if not, the next few pages surely will).

At any rate, for the sake both of clarity and perhaps of new hearing, I choose here to utilize the term *plot* or *plotted* as a way to refer to these several quite different versions of the new homiletic. For those who want to whisper *narrative* as the term *plot* occurs—be my guest. For those who would only be confused, try to ignore the connection. The sermonic plot—related to such plot-forms as the novel, drama, poetry, music, games, and jokes (as well as learning a trade, falling in love, buying a car, taking a trip, and anticipating tomorrow)—is our operational term.

Notice the nature of our strategy when homiletical work is focused in this way. While traditional and kerygmatic type sermons tend to put the magnifying glass on the relationship of ideational construction, sermons of the new homiletic place attention on how people receive ideas. This is consistent with Wilson's advising us to think not of outline but of flow. In another volume I spoke of "doing time" in the pulpit, rather than space.[172] Whereas most of us were taught to organize ideas with listeners close by, we need to understand the sermon as an event-in-time and hence shape people's time with ideational movement.

As evocative event, the sermon's sequence follows the logic of listening, not just the consistency of conceptual categories. Even the issue of the process of coming-to-know is important. Because the preacher has been working on a text and theme for the better part of a week (hopefully), it is tempting to just let the folks in on the conclusions of the preacher's work without repeating the coming-to-know process, but such a process is basic to evocation.

Sermon plots may be shaped by discursive reasoning, poetic imagery, parable, or descriptive material—and in remarkably different modalities—plots of tightly heightened torque or of pleasantly playful incompleteness (and everything in between). Worth noticing in all this is how the sequencing logic differs in significant ways with these various forms of what Rose calls "transformational preaching" and Buttrick calls "plotted mobility." Such great variety shares a unity of purpose—to delay, to withhold, to hide, to keep in abeyance, some basic crucial key, ingredient, striking image, piece of knowledge, or clue, without which nothing can be resolved.

Notice the Variety. The *narrative sermon* most likely will produce an ever-increasingly difficult bind, which moves toward the apparently impossible—until the surprise of the unanticipated turn happens. Typically, the narrative sermon that moves from conflict toward complication into sudden shift or a decisive turn and finally into resolution, denouement, or unfolding will be marked by a much more tightly linear process than, for example, the episodal sermon.

The *episodal sermon* process may appear to jump almost thoughtlessly from one vignette to another seemingly unrelated one—until the intentional internal logic is exposed. How different from the narrative sermon, which moves with increased tension until there is a final release born of the sudden shift. Likely, the episodal sermon is much more laid-back—perhaps with a descriptive scene coming first, followed by a brief but brisk left-brain theological excursion, and then completed by a story. At the point of the story's punch line, a kind of homiletical electrical charge sweeps back through what at first felt like loose pieces welding them into unity. In the episodal sermon process itself, the modality may involve more wonderment than the grip of tension.

And the *story sermon*'s plot—it all depends on the story, the preacher, and the purpose, but it won't end until the resolution happens. The key to the plotting operation of the sermonic story is, of course, the inclusion of characters, setting, action, and tone—all working out the plot from opening disequilibrium to final resolution. It is often the most metaphoric of the six sermon types.

Frequently a story sermon will utilize listeners' natural interest in a story line—without knowing where it is all going to head. What seem like random incidents in the tale all of a sudden have a payoff that could not be anticipated. No doubt, this is what happened to the lawyer who made the mistake of asking Jesus what the term *neighbor* meant. He was led down a path not of his own choosing, and did not know the bottom line until it was too late. Indeed, this sermon type often consists of an elaboration of a parable of Jesus—or for the unusually talented, it may even involve the creation of a contemporary parable.

The apparently traditional *transconscious African American sermon* seems to be marching to a different rhetorical drummer altogether—exegeting, interpreting, and applying the text in careful deductively shaped explanatory form. Except that under-

neath this ideational process is an increasing sense of expectation—growing, swelling, until finally bursting into celebration.
But it must not come too quickly, else the plot won't work
well—so the preacher is advised to "take your time."

The four R's of black preaching described by McClain as
"rhetoric, repetition, rhythm, and rest"[173] all are strategic sequencing strategies that serve as cues for delay and anticipation. They
form a homiletical liturgy that functions to shape the growing
crescendo. Sometimes there is an ideational moment or an image
that goes by without much notice until later when it becomes the
catalyst for the culminating event.

With the *phenomenological move sermon*, it all depends on which
of the three modes are chosen. Whether resembling a story sermon (in the mode of immediacy) or a reflective piece of theological ruminating, nonetheless, the whole sermon will be plotted.
"The word *plot*," says Buttrick, "may be applied to all kinds of
hermeneutical acts; it is not restricted to stories."[174]

The "reflective mode" phenomenological move sermon is
noteworthy by the fact that it consists of a "series of rhetorical
units"[175] in which, says Buttrick, "we are no longer bound by the
original sequence of a passage."[176] What determines the order of
the text as shaped within the sermon has to do with the differing
potential strategies of the preacher.

The telling principle of the *inductive sermon*—as we know by
now—is the arrangement of ideas, moving from particular to
general. But how the particulars are formed may involve quite
different configurations. Sometimes the inductive sermon works
by an accumulation of data that finally overflow into conclusion—not known before. Or again, an inductive sermon may
utilize the juxtaposition of images that will finally "land" with a
surprising twist. Whatever the method, the common sequencing
strategy is to lure listeners toward an unfolding that cannot be
totally anticipated.

The potential forms are endless; the principle singular: delay,
working incompleteness, anticipation, suspense and, one hopes,
resolution born of the gospel. On occasion one may even perceive
a plot happening in a three-point traditional sermon, when point
three becomes not simply the third ramification or form or divi-

sion of the central theme, but the decisively named under-standing that unifies and completes the process.

Hence. The immediate task that lies in front of us now is to move through the stages that often occur in plots. We draw on the somewhat stylized summary of Aristotle's ideas about plot as discussed in *Poetics.* But for this to be very helpful, we will need to use our imagination, stretch his categories, and avoid narrow literalistic construals in our appropriation of his thought.

So now we turn to such plotting processes as conflict, complication, peripeteia (or reversal or sudden shift) and denouement (or resolution or unfolding).

1. Conflict

Conflict is basic to the plotting of a sermon. At the same time, varieties as well as degrees of conflict deserve attention. Buttrick advises the preacher to learn to ask the right questions of a biblical text—namely, to search for "the field of concern." Something is always "lurking," he says.[177] The result of this kind of thinking is not just to name a text's concluding "point," but to what the passage "is trying to do."[178]

Similarly, the great preacher and teacher Edmund Steimle is clear that "if a sermon is to be biblical at its deepest level, it will draw us into the development of a plot . . . the end of which is still in doubt."[179] Although he may have intended the expanded meaning, it may be important to note that sometimes the issue has less to do with the "end of the matter," which is in doubt, and more to do with the yet to be discerned "means" of the matter.

Otherwise put, sometimes the issue of doubt is not *destination* but *route* toward the destination. For example, listeners in Christian congregations are generally confident that we will wind up affirming the power of Christ adequately to usher the community of faith into God's future. The question is precisely how might that happen. The uncertainty is not *what* but *how.* With almost tongue in cheek, I sometimes suggest to students to get Jesus in enough trouble that it becomes unclear (for a while) whether he can get the necessary salvific work accomplished.

Again, congregations naturally expect that we will assent to the authority of the Scriptures. But interim questions often provide potential conflict. And the bottom line of a scripture passage may be quite clear to everyone from the moment it is read. In which case, the preacher might need to find another text that will ask tough questions of the first passage. (Craddock has immense skill in finding just the text that will begin to do battle with another.)

The key term to be used here might be *sideways*. Something has to turn sideways, or the sermon doesn't effectively commence. Given many of the lectionary committee selections, it is not always easy to get sideways of "wonderfully affirmative" doxological texts; it is, however, always required. If you find yourself working with what seems to be a dull, obvious, pedestrian—maybe even overused and hence trite—moralism for a text, it is time to snoop around a bit. Perhaps there is another pole, another level of truth or angle of view that will help get things sideways. Look for what is lurking. Certainly, the funeral sermon does not require extraordinary talent in finding situational conflict.

Rather than speaking of conflict, Paul Scott Wilson likes to speak of imagination that involves "the bringing together of two ideas that might not otherwise be connected and developing the creative energy they generate."[180] And how does one unleash the imagination? By asking questions of the text, he says. "Imagination requires a gap between the text and ourselves so there can be a spark."[181] "Questions," as Wilson imagines them, "are like wild flowers bursting on the hillside, providing wonder and mystery, both of which are necessary for imagination." Apparently, he notes, some people do not "allow themselves" to ask such simple questions as, for example, how it was that Jesus knew Zacchaeus's name. And when you do not ask even small questions like that one, you "have unknowingly trampled the flower of imagination."[182]

So, we are helped here by Wilson in two significant ways. First, he has named a critical means of launching sermon preparation. Second, he has helped us at this point in our consideration to perceive how Aristotle's sense of opening conflict of the plot may be interpreted broadly, and in ways that might otherwise not be noticed. Indeed, imagination is a form of conflict—introducing ambiguity and hence tension in the preacher. Perhaps that may be why some do not "allow" it. Closure does have a sense of security to it, even as it may also become a kind of death grip on the mind and spirit.

The preacher, after all, like other artists, must have a kind of thirst for chaos (a point to which we will return in the chapter on sermon preparation). Ricoeur looks to metaphor as "the birthing room of meaning."[183] Again, as with Wilson's imagination, Ricoeur's metaphor is not usually considered a form of conflict, but that is in fact what the "tease" of metaphor involves. "Metaphor has power by virtue of tension," Buttrick reminds us, "the tension of likeness and dissimilarity."[184]

With Lucy Rose's view of preaching as conversation one might believe that we are far away from the notion of opening conflict, particularly considering her emphasis on a nonhierarchical "round-table church."[185] But when she starts talking about a "wager," you can begin to feel the sense of risk, of vulnerability. After all, where, precisely, does a conversation begin? Certainly not at the point of closure—not with a three-point declaration.

Conversations begin with Kermode's tick, not his tock—a tick launched by the indefinite: "How are things going with the building project?" or "Is your husband doing better now?" kinds of starts. Conversations begin not with the known, the settled, the secure, the fixed, but with the unknown, the unclear, the tenuous, the fluid. A sense of dis-ease or wonderment will get things going—sometimes by what seems to be the smallest of issues.

Now, of course, things are made easier if the text happens to be a biblical story. "There were two who went to the temple to pray. The first said, 'I thank God that . . .' " And we're off and running, doing exactly what Charles Rice said we would—leaning forward, "bending toward" the speaker.[186] But most of the time we are not so lucky. After all, it is quite possible that our next sermon on the Trinity will not immediately draw the congregation forward to the edge of their pews. That is, not until we find the issue, the slight dent in the image, the possible ambiguity.

(With the Trinity as sermon subject, the context of the Garden of Gethsemane might not be a bad place for some serious questions to be found lurking.)

All of which raises a relevant question: If perceived conflict of some kind—and obviously experienced by the listeners, not just the preacher—begins the typical sermonic plot, then what about important texts and topics that do not grab and drag the parishioners to church each Sunday morning? Are we not limiting the scope of preaching fare to the range of people's natural interests? Are we not setting ourselves up for a needed lecture by Karl Barth about the discontinuity between people's perceived concerns and the concerns of the Bible? After all, "if the congregation brings to church the great question of human life and seeks answer for it," Barth once said, "the Bible contrariwise brings an answer, and seeks the question corresponding to this answer."[187]

Certainly it is true that the lazy preacher might be limited to up-front needs and wants—as understood by the people. In ways no different from other aspects of pastoral functioning, those who want to be limited by others' definition of importance will no doubt do so. Yet even in the "democracy" of Rose's conversational preaching, the preacher is the first to speak—and often the only one to speak on that occasion.

This matter can be observed in the related field of drama. I go to the theater expecting an experience not likely continuous with the previous three hours of my life. I pay my money, take my seat, and discover we are in London. We gave no permission, filled out no questionnaires about our perceived concerns, wants, and desires. The playwright appears to have the operative agenda. Later we will be in the driver's seat, but not now.

Nor did an emcee advance to center stage immediately prior to the play, noting that since it is Friday evening and theater goers do look a bit weary from what was no doubt a hard week, the play will be altered by a newly designed beginning, which will take into proper account the particularities of our situation. No, with the competencies of a good playwright, fine director, and skilled actors, we will be lured into a "willing suspension of disbelief" (as they say). The curtain opens and we *are* in London.

Hear Walter Brueggemann in *Finally Comes the Poet* make it clear:

The event of preaching is an event in transformed imagination. Poets, in the moment of preaching, are permitted to perceive and voice the world differently, to dare a new phrase, a new picture, a fresh juxtaposition of matters long known. Poets are authorized to invite a new conversation with new voices sounded, new hearings possible. The new conversation may end in freedom to trust and courage to relinquish. The new conversation, on which our very lives depend, requires a poet . . . [because] places of resistance and embrace . . . are not ultimately reached by instruction . . . [but] only by stories, by images, metaphors, and phrases that line out the world differently, apart from our fear and hurt. The reflection that comes from the poet requires playfulness, imagination, and interpretation. The new conversation allows for ambiguity, probe and daring hunch.[188]

All of this is not to say that Schlafer was wrong to claim that preaching is "more listening than speaking,"[189] and that listening to the congregation is utterly mandatory. Carefully, he speaks of "engaging the various voices,"[190] not just listening. Nor was Forsyth wrong to claim that the church speaks to the preacher, too, and not just the other way around. No, indeed. Quite frankly, there are some claim-to-be-prophets whose authority seems granted by the preacher's own commitment never to listen.

Rather, it is that the connection between pew and pulpit is never that of a "want-say" relation. The proper understanding of the preaching office includes listening to the people *and* listening to the text—along with such other voices as found within the congregation, the cultural environment, the liturgy, and even within the preacher too. The preacher's interpretive responsibilities are large indeed. As Schlafer puts it: "Preaching cannot be *less* than good listening, but it needs to be *more*."[191] Exactly so—born as it is from the depths of pastoral and prophetic sensibilities.

2. Complication

Then, as the saying goes, "Now the plot thickens." Whatever the particular form of the new homiletic sermon, once conflict happens, things always get worse—and in such diverse ways. At least that is the way the plot form should work.

We are accustomed to this basic movement of plot as it happens in other art forms. Often such movement brings real pleasure.

Mozart is quietly playing a pleasant and simple rendition of "Twinkle, Twinkle, Little Star"—and then the music shifts modality. Numerous variations lure us successively into the lighthearted and intimate dance, the slow minor key walk, and the heavy-handed and stately march. Very clever. Quite interesting.

Agatha Christie leads us around the circle at the retreat center placing the mantle of suspicion on first one and then another of the guests in *The Mousetrap*. Why, any of them could be the villain, and all might be the next victim. Very engaging, and apparently very confusing to the detective who is trying to solve the murder mystery—until all at once everything shifts radically. How utterly shocking! We've been taken for quite a ride, and we feel deliciously foolish for having been fooled so well.

Before we leave *The Mousetrap* though, we ought to note the interim period involved—between the first murder and the final reversal. It occupies virtually the entire play and is the *complication*. The opening conflict is murder number one, having occurred elsewhere. As we are getting better acquainted with the cast of remarkable characters, the second murder happens right at the retreat house—right in the darkness before our very eyes. Now, the complication begins running ever more deep because now everyone's life is at stake until the mystery is solved. Such complication. The term *engaging*, however, is appropriate only if our lives are not at stake. So now, let us change the scene.

Jesus and his closest friends are heading up the mountain. They have ever so recently heard his unbelievable announcement regarding his future. One text says the disciples were "heavy with sleep but kept awake"[192] (which sounds like clinical depression to me). Certainly, such a response would be appropriate after their leader announces his impending demise, anticipating his being rejected and killed as a political foe. And then they are told not to tell anyone.

They arrive at the top of the mountain to have what some preachers quite strangely have called a mountaintop experience. (If this is a mountaintop experience, leave me out of it.) The subject of the conversation and action is centered solely on the subject of death, and then they come down the mountain into the middle of human need, and then up another mountain called

Golgotha—to the throes of divine suffering. This particular section of the passion plot is complication indeed, and no one calls it entertaining. It is not simply that it is a plot of incredible tragedy, but also that it is told in the context of a people who know they are somewhere in the middle of that plot.

One does not have to wonder long why some preachers want to avoid this part of the plot. It is so much easier to "close the case" with an exhortation about the duty of discipleship or, as Brueggemann has put it, to reduce the gospel to the instrumentalism of problem solving "born of a 'managerial' consciousness."[193] Indeed, that might be the consciousness that sees the Transfiguration as a mountaintop experience—you know, helpfully instructive. But of course, it does avoid dancing the edge of mystery.

There is within us, I believe, this natural reluctance to really break things open. Little wonder that very shortly after identifying the text's field of concern, articulating the issue, naming the presenting conflict, often we move quickly to close it down, stop the bleeding, and relieve the pain. It sometimes feels like the pastoral thing to do because life can be tough, after all. But such premature closure turns out to be a Band-Aid on life's tragedy, a momentary diversion from the pain—perhaps even an immunity against hearing the good news.

Several years ago I visited a medical specialist to find the cause of the severe wrist pain I was experiencing. The specialist was torn between the diagnosis of carpal tunnel syndrome and degenerative arthritis—apparently the symptoms were about 50-50. Noting that the therapy for the one condition is the exact opposite of the therapy for the other, I asked which treatment I should follow. "Just wait a while," he said. "When it gets worse we will know which it is and hence what to do for it." Notice, only *after* it gets worse. Complication in a sermon often deepens the grasp of the symptoms of our human malady—to the point when diagnosis can become clear and remedy born of the gospel found.

Sometimes it is easier to watch others fall into this understandable trap of pulling back from the increased torque of complication than it is to observe it in ourselves. One time or another most pastors have wandered in on an adult Sunday school class just at the beginning of the session. Someone is about to define a significant world or community problem in two sentences and then solve it with the third—that often begins with "And if you ask me. . . ." Open/shut; problem/solution. Easy.

Fortunately, however, someone else adds a complicating note to the discussion, perhaps a personal experience or some unexpected research numbers on the issue. Another gains the courage to acknowledge disagreement with the opening point of view, and another notes the similarity of a biblical text. By the time the Sunday school hour is over, the conversation has moved from quick fix answer for even quicker-named problems to a much deeper level of consideration. The engagement has gained particularity and depth. The matter may not have been "solved," but the opening conflict has entered the stage of complication. Right there in the Sunday school class.

Oliver Wendell Holmes once remarked that he "wouldn't give a fig for the kind of simplicity that exists on this side of complexity, but would give the world for the simplicity that exists on the other side of complexity."

Good jazz artists understand exactly what Holmes means. Their improvisation can put Holmes's adage into the medium of sound very powerfully. "What distinguishes superior creative musicians from the mediocre ones of all periods," observes professor Leroy Ostransky, "is the manner in which they create resolutions, and to create resolutions it is necessary to set up irresolution. . . . Poor and mediocre jazzmen will impose problems on themselves, problems of resolution whose answers are already evident in the irresolutions they set up." The key, he says, is not the resolution "however elaborate," but the "inherent intricacy of the irresolution."[194]

In the context of our work, if you can back out of a door you have just walked through, it is likely you have not entered the stage of complication. One must move inside the doorway far enough to have reached some point of no return. Perhaps only then will the matter be positioned such that it is possible to hear the redemptive word of the gospel. Is it not the case that often the sermon of apparently unusual power is also memorable by the fact that during the preparation stage the preacher nearly despaired of ever having anything to say? Sometimes, one needs to get lost before one can be found.

Browne makes it clear: "Creative work always brings creative workers to the edge of an abyss." Moreover, "Great preaching, like great art, cannot be the work of those who know no chaos within them and it cannot be the work of those who are unable to master the chaos within them."[195]

How? There are numerous ways to open greater complication in the sermon—all depending upon such variables as the genre of the text, the nature of the issue, and the kind of sermon form being used.

In my first book on preaching, *The Homiletical Plot,* I identified this stage of the sermon as "analyzing the discrepancy."[196] It is instructive to note some assumptions with which I was working. First, we obviously were in the context of a fairly discursive left-brain homiletical style. I urged everyone to ask, "Why?" Why is the issue present? What lies behind the problematic behavior that needs remedy?

Notice another assumption—namely, that the sermon is centered on a problematic topic, named not by goal but by its preresolutional state. The theme was drawn from either contemporary life or from a biblical text that involved a parallel to contemporary life. One illustration I utilized dealt with the issue of *apathy*, which typically has been described as a "failure to care." People "just don't care"—conventional wisdom decrees. But when the matter was probed, when the question "why?" was asked, and when particulars from the real world were introduced, it became clear—finally—that the issue is not that people don't care; it may just be that people care too much—and hence pull back from becoming even more vulnerable. It began to dawn on me, however, that the diagnostic question "why?" is only one way to complicate a sermonic plot. (And, indeed, sometimes it can become an altogether too privatistic kind of method as well.)

In the sermon "Amazing Grace" Fred Craddock reveals another strategy—his often used technique of "allowing one biblical text to do battle with another." (It *is* always prudent to let the texts do the arguing, instead of the preacher.) Among the texts he used

in the sermon for the purpose of placing the listeners in a conflicting bind was one from the Psalms where the righteous are seen
as blessed (and never hungry) while the wicked are punished—
contrasted with a passage from Matthew, which asserts that the
rain comes on the just and the unjust—together with a Lukan
passage about God being kind to the ungrateful and selfish.[197]

Regarding such establishing of increasing complication: the
undoing of people of straw is never effective, no matter how
knowingly the homiletical victory is claimed. The dilemmatic (if
temporary) situation must be credible. We might notice that
fiction writers keep us engaged by placing characters in decisional moments in which the options as presented are conflicted,
not between good and bad (which is a false conflict) but between
good and good, between bad and bad. Competing claims will
help complicate a plot.

In a story sermon, the plot typically is complicated by moving the characters ever more closely to some decisional moment, the consequences of which become ever more critical.
This principle is seen in the John 8 text in which the "innocent"
question to Jesus about whether or not to stone the adulterous
woman gains increased weight of consequences—but upon
them, not him. They had hoped to put Jesus on the spot. Now
they, their integrity, their reputation, and even their job security are increasingly placed on the line—simply by their original inquiry. They had put him in quite a box, they thought, and
then had the lid pulled down on themselves.

In an inductive sermon, complication may be achieved by the
accumulation of conflictual data, which repeatedly short-circuit
obvious conclusion after obvious conclusion in almost Socratic-
like questioning form. After repeated moments of "not this" and
"not this," the listeners are led through a process of elimination
toward another not-revealed-until-now possibility. Or again, the
inductive sermon may facilitate complication by addition rather
than elimination of data.

Episodal sermons often rely on the strategy of shifting ground
without notice or transition. There must be, however, a high
degree of both trust and skill for this to work because the preacher
is asking for continued listener engagement without "audible

means of support." The trusted preacher may lure the listeners from scriptural text to convenience store in a single leap. The untrusted preacher jumps alone. When all jump together, the result can be wonderfully conflicting.

Narrative sermons tend to use the glue of single-thread connectors to make the jump toward new and unfamiliar territory—and hence further complication. The symphonic musical score does it so easily. One movement is coming to an end. The listeners expect dead silence. But when the conductor grandly sweeps the arms of conclusion, one oboe holds out with a single note—the fifth tone of the concluding chord, which by musical magic also just happens to be the third tone of the key of the next moment. The move to greater and fresh complication hangs on the thread of a single oboe tone. (Translation: never make transitions by means of broad conclusions, but with the strength of a powerfully thin note of ambiguity.)

Nobody in our homiletical world knows better the conflicting power of silence than the African American preacher, who holds the congregation literally in midsentence so well that the congregation nearly begs for the move to be made so that the complication can finally be resolved. Or again, the "hum thought" as Evans Crawford describes it, the "sonic materialization of . . . insight and rapture."[198] Notice how such complication works when the African American preacher says what could be ordinarily said, but instead, shapes the thought in such extraordinary fashion as to lure the congregation into increased wonderment and expectation. Instead of a simple reference to the sun, the preacher says, "I looked and saw the first thin pencil line of dawn, and watched God's ball of fire seek its noon meridian, continue its relentless journey to the twilight and then lay down to sleep beyond the western hills."[199]

Whatever the forms of complication in whatever sermonic types, the critical key is the *move to fluidity* where matters are not indefinite, but yet clearly are indeterminate. The movement at this stage of the plot must be movement toward the actually irresolute, the truly dilemmic, the really bound. The task is not in learning how to be clever. That will stick out like a sore thumb. The task is that of moving toward the articulateness of deep silence out of which comes a new word. As the New Revised Standard Version has it at the entrance to Elijah's cave: "a sound of sheer silence."[200]

How one decides about the various options of complicating the plot hinges on a number of factors, but none more important than a concurrent decision also being made in the preparation process. (I say "concurrent" although it is sometimes prior, and sometimes subsequent.) David Schlafer calls this decision "Discerning a Strategy of Integration."[201] He explains:

> The Scriptures engage our senses and our emotions directly by means of images. They also invite us to enter as participants in stories—historical, fictional, and mythical narratives. They further confront us with arguments—orderly presentations of evidence intended to lead us to certain conclusions.[202]

Schlafer believes that after listening carefully to the various voices of text, congregation, liturgy, culture, and self, one of the first steps in sermon preparation is to decide whether the sermon-to-be will be integrated by means of argument, story, or image. It is not that any text has only one of these factors; it is that one will become the dominant means of sermonic shape. Although we will return to his remarkably helpful advice in the next chapter on sermon preparation, it is important now to heed the consequences of this strategy.

We might observe, for example, that how one complicates a plotted sermon based on the strategy of *image* is quite different from complicating an *argument*-based sermon, and different yet from complicating a *story*-based plot.

Imagine the difference even of biblical texts themselves at this point. In Galatians, Paul complicates the plot of his letter by heady argument over the issue of freedom in Christ. It's a dogfight for Paul with his passion swelling to angry eloquence, heading down to hard-hitting logic, and then back up again.

Then there is Jesus telling the tale of a son's move away from home—and whose journey gets complicated by bad weather, worse friends, and a Gentile farmer's pigs. Different yet is the psalmist's imaging of God as shepherd whose providential care includes lush pastures and crystal clean water—but whose vision of reality perceives also the complicating vistas of deathly valleys and ever-present enemies.

While story- and argument-based sermon plots are more easily understood, image-based sermons may need clarification. I have found Patricia Wilson-Kastner helpful in explaining that "imagery means more than pictures; it includes the whole physical and sensory dimension of the world portrayed in a sermon." While "imagery is a more encompassing term than images," sometimes a single image will bring the sensory dimension to focus.[203] So it is with the psalmist's use of the "shepherd" image.

Notice even the different emotions one can imagine and convey—the *anger* of the either-or squabble between Paul and the Galatians, the *lament* of Jesus in the tragic story of the two boys, and the *serenity* encouraged by the psalmist's hope. Choosing a basic strategy from among the three options of image, argument, and story depends partly, but not conclusively, on the literary genre of the text. Sometimes it becomes determined by the purpose of the sermon—or again by the nature of the congregation.

For example, Helmut Thielicke's sermon based on the story of the Pharisee and the publican obviously grew out of a narrative text. Thielicke's strategy of integration, however, clearly did not. Rather, the strategy took the form of argument. How one determines which strategy to utilize will be explored in the next chapter on preparation. For now it is clear that the plotted sermon of whatever kind will follow the opening conflict with increasing complication—until something really decisive happens.

3. Sudden Shift

Just naming this peculiar moment in the sermon's plot is an exercise not only in attempted accuracy of definition, but also toward consistency of theology. Something happens abruptly, decisively. The classical term for this is *peripeteia*, meaning reversal or sudden shift. The designation *decisive turn* might capture it—as long as the turn wasn't gradual.

All of which is why the plot line when visualized:

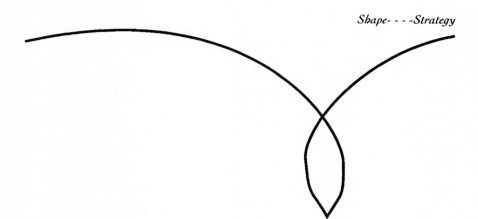

always has a point at the bottom to suggest the radical shift of direction the process takes—not a gradual sweeping curve. We are talking about a sudden seeing here—or is it a sudden hearing? Roth, although for a different reason, prefers the term *recognition*.[204]

In *The Homiletical Plot*, I described a point of reversal that happens in a plot at least three-fourths of the way into the sermon. Until then the "process moves with increasingly felt 'necessity' toward some kind of release, toward the revealing of the missing link. Once disclosed, matters are seen in a different light."[205]

In *Doing Time in the Pulpit*, I described how increased complexity and heightened suspense move us to the point when "by means of reversal, a new profound simplicity overtakes the confusion."[206] This view is certainly consistent with Aristotle, who spoke of a "reversal of the situation . . . , a change by which the action veers round to its opposite."[207]

Yet, several adjustments appear now in order. Although the decisive turn is sometimes a direct reverse of the previous point of view—or often the *presumed* previous point of view—this is not always the case. Just as John Dominic Crossan names "parables of reversal" as one among three types of parables,[208] so it is readily apparent that not all plotted sermons involve a polar reversal of a one-hundred-eighty-degree turn. Were we to employ the term *reversal* in simplistic fashion, many texts, themes, and occasions would be unwittingly excluded.

Perhaps the best way to explore this decisive moment in the sermon process is to describe *reversal* or *peripeteia* in its most radical—we shall not say *pure*—form. Then we will consider the kind of less radical form this sudden shift may appropriately take in the work of preaching.

Jesus' use of parables was not simply a matter of "good pedagogical strategy," says Amos Wilder, but because of "something in the nature of the Gospel."[209] Wilder is referring here to the fact that life has about it the character of a plot. Jesus' parables have a revelatory function. Unlike the term *discovery, revelation* by definition includes a sense of apparent discontinuity. It happens, after which everything takes on new meaning.

Is it not true that the gospel is a "yes" to the world's "no," that the "last will be first, and the first last,"[210] that "those who seek to save their life shall lose it"[211]? The very genre of parable itself captures this "eventive" sense of revelation. Indeed, the parable of the good Samaritan is a reversal twice. First, it takes the good-bad assumption of *Jew-Samaritan* and reverses it to *Samaritan-Jew.* Second, it shifts definitions of *neighbor* from *person-in-the-ditch* when we enter the parable to *person-helping-person-in-the-ditch* when we leave the parable.[212]

This kind of startling reversal can be found in all kinds of secular literature—for example, when with Shakespeare, the story begins with everyone having sight except for the blind man. When the story is completed, everybody is blind except for the blind man who, singularly, has vision. Likewise, when the story of the man born blind who was healed by Jesus on the Sabbath is concluded, one religious leader asks, "Are we blind too?"[213]

Functioning exclusively in the theological world of narrowly defined reversals, however, is not only difficult but ultimately so restrictive as to become false to the whole gospel—seems to me. There is a kind of tightly construed either-or, Christ against culture sectarianism that would turn Jesus into a modern-day zealot and the church into a ghetto.

The zealous—gospel as reversal only—disciples who desired fire to rain down upon a Samaritan village found Jesus' quick response to include not only rebuke, but a parable in which a Samaritan was the hero. Either-or construals may bring with them the ease of sharp definition and sometimes the pleasure of quick certainty. And it always unpacks the poem. But the world is not always so clear. Dancing the edge of mystery is another matter altogether. And it is nuanced with greater humility as well.

Moreover, any model of sermon shape must be fluid enough to be widely usable, yet not so general as to lose definability. Some sermons will in fact turn a polar reversal at the point of the sudden shift. Most, however, are not so radical. What is important is that the turn be so decisive that there is no way to go back to the previous view. For example, after Bartimaeus is healed, Jesus tells him to "go." But he doesn't go—if you mean to go back to the usual spot on the roadway of Jericho from which he came. Bartimaeus doesn't *go;* he *comes.* He joins the crowd accompanying Jesus and, presumably, follows Jesus into Jerusalem.[214] There is another decisive turn in the story. Now that Bartimaeus can see, he has no choice but to look—even as Jesus heads toward the cross. The shift is fundamental; it is, yet, not a polar reversal.

Quite outside the context of biblical story, decisive homiletical turns also occur. We considered one earlier in this chapter that was a shift of rationality (concerning the issue of apathy and its cause). I believe it fair to suggest that Paul's description of the relation of law to gospel is variously described—all the way from the polar reversal stance of the law as a covenant of condemnation—"the curse of the law"—to the less than over-and-against view of the law as custodian—"our disciplinarian until Christ came." Both comparisons of law and gospel come from the same chapter of the same Pauline writing.[215]

Other biblical stories share the kind of sharp and suddenly decisive shift that, while not technically a polar reversal, nonetheless leaves us torn away from prior perception into a new way of thinking that changes everything. For example, the story of the widow's stewardship contains in bold relief numerous opposites. Others have much; she has little. They give relatively little; she gives all. Their financial status is essentially unchanged; her financial status has undergone a revolution. They leave with their pockets still full; she departs with an empty purse. They are still full and she is now empty. Or is it in fact the other way around, with their leaving the treasury empty while she leaves full?[216]

Or again, Jesus is led into the wilderness where the devil is going to work him over. Does it not seem strange that he was led not by the devil, but by the Spirit? And the temptations are the reverse of what one might expect. He was not being lured into lascivious, debased living as the preachers of my youth always describe the matter. No, he was asked to turn stones into bread—and in a country where there were too many stones and too little bread. Does this seem to you a temptation—or is it more of an opportunity for ministry?[217]

Again, the key is the abruptness of the moment of the shift and the luminous nature of the insight that seems to shut the door behind itself. Some are polar reversals; others come in turns of less than one hundred eighty degrees. As a result, I prefer the term *sudden shift* as the way to describe this stage of the sermon. It is—to think by analogy—the moment in the detective story when the culprit is named. In the A-A-B-A musical sequence of a typical ballad, it is the moment between B and A, when after a shift of key, of melodic line, and of verse motif (called the bridge), the music restates the theme another time—a theme transformed by the route it has just traveled.

I also think the timing of this sudden shift is crucial. In an earlier writing I suggested the turn happens about three-fourths into the sermon. Perhaps five-sixths is better. On rare occasions it may happen on the last line. Most generally, preachers tend to allow it to happen too quickly. I disagree with Paul Scott Wilson who wants us to divide the sermon into two halves—with "a fifty-fifty balance between law and gospel."[218] I certainly understand his concern that people carry with them from the worship service the resolution born of grace. But quantity of words is not the appropriate measure. The quality of impact, the suddenness of perception, and the power of decisive insight are central.

In addition to the variety we have just discussed—the variety of degrees of radicality in the sudden shift—there is another kind of variety to the decisive turn—the forms that the peripeteia, reversal, or turn may utilize.

Means of the Sudden Shift. Earlier we considered Schlafer's view of discerning a strategy of integration for the sermon, and the three options of image, story, and argument available for carrying the content of the sermon through the stages of the plot.

The same three factors of image, story, and argument play important roles in the decisive peripeteia or turn of the sermon.

One might presume, of course, that in a plotted argument sermon (as Schlafer defines it), a striking piece of logic will prompt the sudden shift, and that—likewise—in a plotted image sermon, a fresh turn of imagery will cause the shift. Often things do work this way—but not always. Sometimes a decisive image may shift a line of reasoning—or a piece of logic may reverse a story line.

For example, the story line of the Jacob narrative is so compelling that a sermon on Jacob will quite likely utilize *story* as the strategy of integration. The movement from one con job to the next fairly well keeps Jacob running on down the road. First the birthright, then the blessing, then the competition with equally astute con artist Uncle Laban, and finally down to the Jabbok river. Everything moves—including the angels on the self-serving ladder—by which Jacob tries to con even God.

Yet, there is an image, a picture the morning after the wrestling match that says it all. Jacob—call him Israel now—walks with a limp. And the limp is for real. After previously placing everyone ahead of him in two lines on the Esau side of the river (while he stays on what he thought was the safe side), and so that all will die before his angry brother gets to him, he now arises in the morning and limps his way past the two groups so that he will be *first* to be confronted by Esau and his four hundred troops.

The dramatic reversal is captured by the limp. He had been running for years as a fractured person. Now he is whole—whole enough to be able to afford the slow, disjointed rhythm of a limped walk. The image of limp can make the decisive turn.

Likewise, my sermon on the workers in the vineyard (the manuscript of which is printed in *How to Preach a Parable*) utilizes a concept—an argument of sorts—to provide the means of the sermon's sudden shift. After joining forces with the early workers who are rightfully offended by such obvious injustice, I searched around to find some factor that might make everything right. After all, I had hoped not to have to oppose Jesus in Sunday's sermon. Surely, there must be a key to some new view of the appalling scene.

I had hunted for some "break" in the previous chapter, when Simon Peter said: "We have left everything to follow you; what do we get?"[219] And somehow in my conversation with the text in that previous chapter, it suddenly dawned on me that my sermon might just hinge on the difference between contracts and covenants. These terms as defined by ordinary dictionaries appear virtually synonymous, but they are remarkably different in real life (like the difference between buying a car and getting married).

Although I never mention the terms *contract* and *covenant*, preferring instead to use the images of *business deal* and *family*, the concept nonetheless was the instrumentality by which the sermon plot line shifted. It is not a polar reversal, but it is a radical one. The point here is to note how discursive thought turned the story line around.

Affirming Roth's description of "recognition" as basic to appropriation of the gospel, it is sometimes the case that a story may provide the sudden sense of being grasped by truth in a powerful and newly gestaltive form. Toni Craven cites James Paul Gee who notes how the telling of a story may make an event real. Gee claims, for example, that medieval Muslim historians did not use the term *Crusade* because "no such event as a Crusade [was] taking place."[220] The Crusades were not the Crusades, but conflicts with ordinary enemies until the middle 1940s when "Arabic writers . . . tell a different story" based on a newer perception of colonization that had been going on for centuries.[221] Once a narrative pattern was recognized, the Crusades came to life—according to Gee.

Gabriel Fackre, in writing about narrative theology, notes the three levels of story that are engaged: canonical story, life story, and community story.[222] I believe that the interweaving of these three levels of story—canonical, life, and community—is crucial for the church in general and the sermon in particular. Whether the pastor uses the integrative strategy of story, argument, or image, the result may indeed evoke that sudden shift prompting what Craddock calls the "shock of recognition."[223] Sometimes it is a story that evokes it—whatever the basic sermon strategy. When it does, the sudden shift happens.

Relation of Sudden Shift to the Good News. So far in this chapter we have described how the plotted sermon moves from opening conflict or discrepancy through increased complication into some kind of sudden shift or reversal that changes everything. Elsewhere I have spoken of this plot form as the movement from *itch* to *scratch*.

We also know that a sermon's move toward final resolution or unfolding is shaped around the claim of the gospel of Jesus Christ. Ours is not simply the bad news task of moral exhortation, of pushy nit-picking for people to do better because Jesus wants it so. No, we are talking good news here. Of course, it makes a claim upon us (which we will yet consider in the next section of this chapter), but it is a claim based on promise. There can be no *imperative claim* without the *indicative* based on the Good News of Christ. Otherwise, we are pushing an ethics of obedience message only. So, Wilson speaks of law moving to gospel.

The question, therefore, is: Where and how does the indicative, the good news, appear in the plot line? In graph form, the plot looks like this:

Conflict _ _ _ > Complication _ _ _ > Sudden Shift _ _ _ > Unfolding

Where does the good news show up?

When I wrote *The Homiletical Plot*, the question seemed a bit simpler to me than it does now. And I had five stages or steps—not four—in the plot sequence. It went like this:

Oops _ _ _ _ > Ugh _ _ _ _ > Aha _ _ _ > Whee _ _ _ _ > Yeah

Upsetting *the* *Equilibrium*	*Analyzing* *the* *Discrepancy*	*Disclosing* *the* *Clue to* *Resolution*	*Experiencing* *the* *Gospel*	*Anticipating* *the* *Consequences*

Often this sequence as described here is exactly right. That is, the stage of complication ("analyzing the discrepancy," I called it then) often involves the analytic work of asking "why?" If the sermon subject is apathy (a theme discussed in "The Plot") and we discern that apathy typically does not arrive out of "not caring," but out of "caring too much" (a reversal of presumed causality) and with the newly focused clue becoming fear of failure, then such suddenness of surprising analytic shift opens the door immediately to the good news. It announces the love of Christ—particularly for those who consider themselves failures. The sermon's promise of the good news, then, properly unfolds into the possibility of a newly shaped future in which the surprise of God's unconditional love results in the miracle of empowerment—even our new capacity to risk future failure.

Or again, Helmut Thielicke's sermon on the Pharisee and the publican reveals the same basic plot line—this time utilizing a biblical story. After Thielicke hooks the listeners *(Oops)* by noting that such an apparently simple story actually is not so simple after all, and that the truth is that the Pharisee was in fact as good as he claims and the publican as bad as he admits *(Ugh)*, how could it be that the "wrong" man went home justified (further complication). The plot line is easy to discern here. After keeping the listeners hanging on his detailed explanation of Pharisee and publican—their differences and their commonalties—finally, he says: "We hit upon the salient point."[224] One can almost hear the congregation in relief shout *"Aha!"* And the salient point? It is that "if you want to know yourself you must have a standard. . . . The Pharisee measures himself by looking downward when he tries to determine his rank before God."[225] Bingo!

Well now, if the issue—as properly analyzed—is the downward glance in order to feel better about oneself, we are not far from claiming the good news, that God's incredibly gracious love removes the need for such a downward glance—that Christians do not need an ego boost by means of noticing "lesser" people. Hence, because the burden of self-rejection is healed, life can be utterly different. Note that in both these cases, the good news falls in place precisely *after* the sudden shift of analysis discloses the surprising clue to resolution.

Conflict – – – > Complication – – – > Sudden Shift – – – > Unfolding
Good News

But alas, not all texts and topics in preaching work this way. For example, the parable of the workers in the vineyard (to once again follow my treatment of that text as it is found in *How to Preach a Parable*) happens differently. The complicating analysis doesn't result in a sudden shift. It draws matters into an ever-tightening dilemmic bind. The more consideration given to the questions of relative justice, the clearer it becomes that the hero (vineyard owner) is not only crass (paying the last ones first) and obviously unethical; indeed, he is also stupid because tomorrow, when he goes to the marketplace at 6:45 A.M. to hire workers, nobody will come forward; workers *will* be available about 4:45 in the afternoon.

No sudden shift here. It was as I probed around in the previous chapter, happening to come across Simon Peter's selfish question: "We have left everything to follow you; what do we get?" that it happened. I realized that the only proper answer to such a selfish question is "Well, cheated, of course." Anyone so crass as to think of the reign of God as a business deal is way off base. The *Aha* is that we are not invited to *duty*—earn as we go. We are God's *family* who have been invited home. Now, that's altogether different—radically different. Note: the sudden shift didn't happen first, in order to open the door for the gospel. The sudden shift *is* the good news. *Rather than:*

Conflict _ _ _ > Complication _ _ _ > Sudden Shift_ _ _ > Unfolding
$\wedge$
Good | *News*

that fits our first two sermon examples (on apathy and the Pharisee and the publican) *with this example of the workers in the vineyard,* it is:

Conflict _ _ _ > Complication _ _ _ > Sudden Shift_ _ _ > Unfolding
$\wedge$
Good | *News*

There is yet a third option. Earlier we discussed blind Bartimaeus. Blindness with its accompanying marginality is the opening *conflict. Complication* includes his crying out for mercy, the townspeople telling him to shut up, Jesus asking what he wanted—if it were not clear enough. The basic good news happens immediately without fanfare or sudden shift; Jesus heals him and tells him to go his way. The *sudden shift* is his not returning to his place in Jericho, but instead, joining Jesus' followers who together are heading to Jerusalem. Hence, in this case the plot looks like this:

Conflict – – – > Complication – – – > Sudden Shift– – – > Unfolding

Good ˄ News

It would be simpler if all *argument* sermons followed the first plan with *story* sermons following the second and *image* sermons following the third. But it is just not the case. Or again, do all *episodal* sermons always work one way and inductive sermons another? Certainly, I think there may be tendencies.

For example, episodal-style preaching sometimes has the sudden shift right at the sermon's conclusion. Craddock often walks away from the pulpit just *before* what we thought would be his final sentence. The sudden shift of African American sermons also generally happens close to the end. Yet, there are no absolutes here. (And we will talk further about this issue in the next chapter.)

This business about relating the good news and the sudden shift is not as complicated as it may seem at this moment. What is important is the preacher's concentration in preparation not on the final naming of the good news, but on the search for the sudden shift. Once found, it will by its nature "tell" the preacher whether it should come before, at, or after the good news. (The practice is in fact easier than the explaining.)

For now, we need to press forward toward unveiling the last section of the plot—the *unfolding.* We will explore several constants regarding this final portion of the plotted sermon, commonalities that are important to name. Once we get the whole plot revealed—*conflict, complication, sudden shift,* and *unfolding*—we will be able in the chapter on sermon preparation to gain further clarity regarding important variations that are possible.

4. Unfolding

Having considered the first three stages of a sermonic plot, *conflict, complication,* and *sudden shift*—and noted how the good news happens either at or nearby the point of the sudden shift—we are ready to explore the final stage of the sermon. Just exploring the process and noting the choice of terms in naming this homiletical stage will facilitate its definition.

In *The Homiletical Plot,* I referred to this concluding section as "anticipating the consequences," a very apt and accurate designation—except for one small problem. The term *consequences* does carry some unnecessary freight. I remember as a child my parents often referring to consequences; they were never happy ones. What I really meant by "anticipating the consequences" is anticipating the future result of the interface of human dilemma and gospel promise. Paul understood that there are consequences to such an interaction: "What then are we to say about these things?"[226] His answer is that "if God is for us, who is against us?"[227] The forms of the question are endless: What now? What should be done? What now is possible? Brueggemann understands it both as a wonderfully "odd invitation"[228] and as an "opening for newness."[229]

The traditional, technical term for this concluding section of a plot is *denouement*. The term actually means "unraveling"—not of the plot, but of the suspense generated by the plot. Again, this is an apt description. Any good plot increases in suspense, in expectation, in wonderment. When matters finally come together in *resolution* (another appropriate term), the tension dissipates toward a newfound state of dynamic equilibrium.

Yet, the term *equilibrium* must be carefully defined. We are not talking here about inactivity, the stasis born when opposing forces are made equal. We are talking about the equilibrium of a runner in stride. This stage has about it the concluding balance of energy that no longer is trapped by fighting a standoff battle. We are now ready to move into the future. We might just continue with Paul who now asks whether God "who did not withhold his own Son, but gave him up for all of us, will he not with him also give us everything else?"[230] (One can feel the rhythm of Paul's stride leaning into the future.)

Nor does the sense of resolution mean all is well in the world and relaxation is now allowed. Some people are unnecessarily nervous that plot means, finally, a cheap, happy solution where all are made ready for a night of pleasant dreams. No, the gospel has to do not with "mastering . . . complexity," says Browne, "but of bearing it."[231] What preaching hopes to evoke is a moment that "breaks open old worlds,"[232] as Brueggemann articulates it. The final stage of the sermon attempts to set the real world stage for the future—both the power to confront the nightmare and the trust to risk the vulnerability of sleep. Paul continues, "Who will separate us from the love of Christ? Will hardship, or distress, or persecution, or famine, or nakedness, or peril, or sword?"[233] One way or another, the promise continues to be made, sermon after sermon, text after text, occasion after occasion, that "we are more than conquerors through him who loved us."[234]

The selection of the term *unfolding* is my attempt to capture the firm liveliness of the promise as named again in the sermon's final words. This is, after all, the sermonic scratch to its previous sermonic itch—a scratch born of the gospel.

Given the subsiding of tension originally prompted by conflict, exacerbated by complication, and turned radically in the power of the good news, there is not much time left in the sermon. We are at least three-fourths through—perhaps with only a few sentences left. All of which is determined, of course, by the particular nature of text and issue—among other things we will soon mention.

This is a crucial time for powerful economy with words. As tension subsides, the listeners will not abide lots of new material. Rather, this is the time to name quickly and powerfully the consequences of our being claimed by the gospel's prophetic and poetic anticipation of "new possibility in the listening assembly."[235]

Likewise, the preacher names the imperative claim that rides alongside the indicative promise of the gospel. Bartimaeus, now healed, must now look; there is no option. That he now *can* look is the marvelous surprise. And the *imperative* is not riding on the back of the *indicative*. This is no contradictory "conditional-free grace." It simply is successive, subsequent. Once healed of blindness, the community now can see what is uglier than our worst fears as well as what is infinitely lovelier than could be thought possible. And before Paul is through with his letter to the church at Rome, he makes clear the unfolding claim: "I appeal to you therefore, brothers and sisters, by the mercies of God, to present your bodies as a living sacrifice, holy and acceptable to God."[236]

It could be called "settling in to tomorrow." The focus here is anticipated genesis, imagined effect, gracious inducement, expected responding, consequential flowering, surprising releasing, unexpected blossoming—indeed, unfolding. The most likely temptation for the preacher here is the temptation to say *too* much about this result of the gospel's intersection with human life.

Preachers often doubt the quality and integrity of their work, and hence feel obligated to explain—to unpack—what might just have been released. Nervously, we may suggest this specific consequence, these four places for proper application, these two most important challenges to our faithfulness. The congregation feels the unneeded reiteration of duty and feels its integrity being questioned in the process. As an actor once told me—when the play is powerful, people do not want a tour of the building.

Fred Craddock has this wonderful way of return—what I call a "half-reprise." After naming the good news in a process finding satisfaction for that homiletical movement—from increased anticipation through the shock of recognition—he then names the claim, the call for human response explicit in the sermon—but often will not leave it there.

The sermon will not be complete until he reaches back to that earlier section in which the good news was named ever so clearly. In a fashion analogous to the jazz moment at the end of the big band presentation, when someone calls out "one more time," he will ever so deftly, lightly, and suggestively repeat a phrase from that earlier articulation of the good news. This reprise quickly places the message graciously in the lap of the listeners—note, not with imperative claim, but with indicative promise.

How this final portion is shaped depends, of course, on text and issue, preacher and occasion—but also on the basis of the strategy of integration defined by Schlafer. Perceptively, Schlafer notes the difference of preacher-congregation relationship that happens naturally as a result of the choice of strategy from among the options of argument, story, and image.

He says that in the *argument* sermon, the preacher and the congregation seem to be facing each other—dialoguing face-to-face. In the *story* sermon, the preacher and the congregation are alongside each other—walking the journey together. In the *image* sermon, the preacher is standing behind the congregation, pointing at the image source.[237] Hence at the sermon's conclusion, we might imagine a handshake for the more logical sermon—in left-brain agreement. With the story-based sermon, we see the preacher and the congregation walking hand in hand. With the image sermon, we might discover that they have become so drawn by the image as to lose sense of separate identity—having been grasped into what Vivas calls "intransitive attention."[238]

Before concluding our consideration of this final section of the plotted sermon, we might need to notice the different use of a couple of fairly similar terms. You may recall my use in chapter 2 of the term *evocation* in reference to the goal of the preaching task—namely, proclamation. My claim was (and is) that we cannot control the result of our sermons. We do our best, of course, but know that with God's Word, we are at best working provisionally. The Spirit works with certainty. Our task is to try to maximize the possibility of proclamation happening. We simply cannot produce it by will.

The term *unfolding* sounds remarkably similar—suggesting the culminating process of the sermon. But, by contrast, the context of the term *unfolding* is the sermon itself—not its hoped-for result. It is the plot that we as artists have shaped that finally moves toward the future. At the concluding moment of the sermon, the use of the term *unfolding* refers to how we have intended the shaped movement of thought to occur—and obviously in what order. *Evocation* is a reference to what, prayerfully, we hope will by God's grace become the ultimate result. Hence, in combining the terms of the chapter entitled "Task-Goal" with this chapter, the relative meanings are as follows:

unfolding is to sermon *task*
what
evocation is to sermon *goal*

One remembers H. Grady Davis's image of the sermon as a tree, the sense of the unfolding of the plot is clarified. Recalling his insight that preaching happens when there is a generative idea that has its own life and power, one can perceive the modality of partnership in the preaching enterprise. The preacher names the conflict born of the text, then assists it to become ever more complicated. The hope is that by the time of the sudden shift and then the unfolding, that life force is *branching out* in its own way with the preacher's cooperative labor.

We "are authorized to invite a new conversation," says Brueggemann, that "may end in freedom to trust and courage to relinquish."[239] "Relinquish"! Such powerful language has a strange affinity with Eliseo Vivas's image of midwife. Although the life in question is not of our origin or control, our task, finally, is to facilitate an unfolding—hoping that the result of such trusting freedom and relinquishing courage may become the issue of a live birth born of the gospel.

5

PREPARATION ········ PRESENTATION

*T*he bottom-line question is: How does one go about preparing for a sermon that moves in the following plotted form?

Conflict – – – > Complication – – – > Sudden Shift– – – > Unfolding

Answering this question will occupy us for most of this concluding chapter.

Typically, the task of preparing the sermon moves through the broad stages of *attending, imagining,* and *shaping.* All totaled there are ten specific steps to the overall process. The reader will not be surprised when I say that this is not a random grocery list of ten, but a plotted journey.

But before we move through the ten steps, we need to affirm one very important caveat. Namely, the preparation process is different not only among diverse preachers, but also over time for any given preacher. Note that I speak of preparation as it "typically" happens, not as it always should or does. (Likely, there will not be more than these ten steps—sometimes fewer.)

I understand that my friend and onetime colleague Dr. Lee Moorehead during his years in the pastorate always prepared his sermon in one sitting on Thursday. Personally, I cannot work this way, and I find several good reasons not to recommend this practice. However, it works for him—and has for more than forty years. Who am I to complain? That is *not* to say, however, that I *never* complain about forms of preparation. Some hinder effective work—seems to me; others facilitate the process. (I will explain what I mean as we go.)

Likewise, anyone who has preached even for a relatively short period of time knows that occasionally, a sermon will simply happen, when out of the blue, some spark of imaginative thought will take over and—one might say—virtually shape itself. Everyone who preaches long enough will experience some such gift.

Some preachers actually note that—once—a preaching event without any preparation whatever seemed to produce a better sermon than usual. (Which does make one wonder about the "usual.") I have always maintained that such "tempting the Lord" will work twice. By the third time of yielding to this temptation, an ill-advised confidence will cut off the supply of adrenaline which was gracious twice—but never again.

Many times the preparation process will get convoluted with, say, step six coming before step four, yet the exceptions do not undercut the rationale—seems to me. Exceptions can be wonderful, but to have no norm is terrible.

Here, then, are the steps I recommend, which *typically* will help the preacher maximize the chance for the kind of effective preaching that moves into becoming the proclamation of the Word.

Attending

Although from time to time the beginning point for sermon preparation proper starts with a congregational situation or world event, I am presuming that most of the time, we begin with a text or texts. (The principles remain the same either way.)

1. Immersing Oneself in the Text

As strange as it seems, the best approach to sermon preparation is to attempt to set aside the means-end rationality of thinking about Sunday coming. Wallow in the text. Read it out loud. Hear it and see it. The mind works differently through the ear and through the eye. Silent thought and oral speech are quite different perceptual and epistemological realities.

If you have ever tried to state your view on a subject at the request of another, and you became embarrassed by not being clear about what you thought you thought—even after the first, second, and third attempts at trying to say it—and if the other person is about to suggest that you stay quiet until you figure out what you mean, then you have learned a valuable lesson. The lesson is that typically, one doesn't know what one thinks until after hearing one's own voice say it.

Again, do your best to forget that Sunday is coming. Read the text out loud over and over—and in numerous translations and paraphrases. Then say it in your own words. Dive in the deep end of the biblical pool. Get inundated with the biblical word. One thing that quickly becomes noticeable is that when you read out loud, you have to inflect the voice, which shapes the meaning of a phrase.

Did the writer of Luke-Acts in the opening introduction mean for Theophilus to "*know* the truth concerning the things about which you have been instructed," or for Theophilus to "know the *truth* concerning the things about which . . . ?"[240] Which is it? Without reading out loud one might never ask this crucial question that impacts one-quarter of the New Testament writings. One principle for this preliminary thinking about the biblical text is to wander around—somewhat innocently and aimlessly. And why? Because if we don't watch it, we who preach may just take a text over—making it mean what we wanted to say before we opened the book. We need to operate with an ideology of suspicion—aimed directly at ourselves. We know too much, you know.

Although it is unpopular to say so, most of us have a canon within the canon—and often without direct intentionality, it begins to work on the text and on us. If not monitored, it works all too well. This is not at all to suggest that any of us can move into some kind of superior neutral position. Such a position does not exist—and if it did would not be worth considering superior. "Perhaps the one thing we know for certain about preaching," says David Bartlett, "is that it is perspectival. The preacher, like every interpreter of a text, brings his or her history, biases, hopes, and fears to the sermon."[241] So, if Bartlett is correct, what's the point here? We have a bias—always called "commitment" by those who have it—and the bias works. Is this not the natural and unavoidable way things work? Not quite. There is no neutral position, of course, and we are often unaware of some of our biases. Yet, *how* one manages those known biases/commitments is immensely important. The only thing worse than a preacher who is not self-conscious about theological and biblical interpretive principles is the preacher who actually claims not to have any. "I don't interpret the Bible; I just preach it."

To the contrary, it is possible to have points of view to some significant degree monitored by the suspicious self—at least to the point of their not working automatically. Any good police detective knows how to suspend or question assumptions and commitments long enough to become open to a clue otherwise unnoticed.

The point at this beginning stage in the sermon preparation process is to do everything possible to get out of the driver's seat; hence, the terms *attending* and *immersing*. The archaic meaning of the term *communicate* says it wonderfully: "to share in or partake of."[242] Wallow, wander around inside story lines and images and arguments. Be loose; get a feel for it. And the good pastor will not wander around in the texts alone, but with companions of congregation, culture, and liturgy as well. Becoming self-conscious of our own agenda, making a point of temporarily holding in abeyance our deeply considered theological convictions, and finding behaviors that will attempt to sidestep the grip of automatic reactions can be helpful in discovering the freedom to hear a new word.

Right away, the reader may already have guessed that just as I believe the sermon as preached moves from itch to scratch, so also the preparation process needs to move from itch to scratch. We're trying to get free, open, unsettled. Actually, some *confusion* at this point would be most helpful.

As strange as it may seem, the shortest, most effective route to Sunday often begins with what appears to be an unnecessary detour through the territory of difficulty, confusion, and uncertainty. Did not Pablo Picasso once remark somewhere that every act of creation is first of all an "act of destruction"? If we never fell off balance, we would never, ever take a step.

2. *Looking for Trouble*

The title might be overstated, but not by much. After immersing oneself in the text, it is time to get sideways. That is, it is time to find the peculiar—the comment that seems not to flow easily in the passage, the point of view of Jesus that is problematic, the comment by the Pharisee that ought to be appreciated. Perhaps something just feels wrong here—if we could shed our virtue long enough to notice.

Indeed, David Bartlett models exactly the needed attitude. We should notice, he says, that

> all the letters [of Paul] . . . , except perhaps Romans, represent one side of a conversation, and the only side we get to hear. Reading Paul is a little like hearing one end of a telephone conversation. "You foolish Galatians!" he says, but we're not quite sure what they said or did to provide that outburst, and we are quite sure that foolish is not how they would describe themselves.[243]

In one sense, this is not so much a separate step in the process as it is an attitude that is helpful throughout the preparation process. A common thread in the work on creativity during the past twenty-five years in business and industry is the conclusion that one of the reasons problems are not more readily solved and creativity so hard to come by is that people do not notice. They take for granted. As a result, often the newcomer, the person on the margins of the industry, is the most creative. Others know—and hence, assume—too much.

"Stereotyping and labeling are extremely prevalent and effective perceptual blocks," said James L. Adams in *Conceptual Blockbusting.* "One simply cannot see clearly if one is controlled by preconceptions."[244] He could have said: " . . . if controlled by firmly held theological convictions."

For example, Jesus' parable of the rich fool is a good candidate for labeling because it catches us by our virtue. Here is a person who is doing very well—well enough to need bigger barns for storage. He is ready to build them when he gets accosted by God, who calls him a fool. Apparently, summarizes Jesus, his problem is in not being "rich toward God."[245] The story looks simple and obvious. Indeed, it was prefaced by Jesus' remark about greed. It is obviously aimed toward the filthy rich and irreligious—easy for the pious preacher and the flock who surely have met such people. Except, I wonder.

Since I am among the wealthy of the earth, have not chosen to give everything away to the poor or taken a vow of poverty—is it possible that I am included in his critique? Just recently, I was working with others toward a revision of our school's retirement plan—the better to finance my retirement someday. Does Jesus mean it is wrong to plan ahead? I thought concern for tomorrow was called stewardship, not greed. Did he really mean it literally when he said "do not worry about tomorrow"?[246] Well, this parable could be a meddler after all.

Strange things may happen if you look for trouble—the weird, the strange, the out of place. Actually, it is like the child who continually irritates us by asking, "Why? why?" and won't be satisfied with any answer given. It is this mind-set that we will do well to recapture. As strange as it seems, I believe that this mind-set can be cultivated.

I once worked with the late Roger Carstensen in several continuing education courses. He helped students not only understand but become comfortable with thinking "unrighteous" weird and strange thoughts—all outside the vulnerability of formal preaching work. He asked the students to name several cultural proverbs with which many of us have been raised ("the early bird gets the worm" kinds of sayings). After he listed several on the chalkboard, he asked each of us to create a new proverb to replace each of them—just like the ones listed, only different—particularly in reversed form. The results were creative, hilarious, and helpful for preachers in discovering how to go about eliciting new ideas. He called the exercise "Turning the Coin Over."

3. Positioning Oneself to Be Surprised

The truth is, no one can by an act of the will decide simply to be more open to fresh nuances of meaning of the biblical text. On the back of an office door I have a sign that reads: "Be spontaneous now." It doesn't work. This is where it is so easy via the mentality of modernity to go awry. Joel Barker, who for twenty years now has gone around the world talking about paradigm shifts, operates on the notion that if we *know* the problem and *will* to change it, the matter is solved.[247] Such naivete by which we live.

No, one cannot directly choose to hear, see, or touch what one has been missing. But one can choose behaviors that will *maximize* the possibilities of enlarged perception. For example, I am told that one method used by instructors in canvas art for the purpose of assisting students in perceiving the details of a landscape is to require the students to stand on their heads and look at the scene. The fact that the upside-down world is different helps them see things lost by routine perspective.

An equivalent for preachers is to be asked to *underline all the important portions* of the biblical text in question. After the underlining is complete, then the preachers should *look at what was* not *underlined.* It is quite likely that these are the sections being taken for granted. For example, the older brother refuses to come to the party for the prodigal son. And his reasoning—if we notice—is rather convincing. When did you ever throw a party for me?

It does seem unfair for the bad boy, the alienated son, to get the party—with the faithful son's fatted calf no less. Until you look at what we did not underline—which likely is the older brother's parking of the tractor. He seeks out the truth from a servant about the cars in the circle drive. Would it not be the normal thing for him to run in—or drive in—and ask the father directly? Why ask a third party about the balloons? Unless, of course, the elder son is already alienated from the father, too—without ever leaving the farm.

Another method of possibly gaining a new perspective on a text is to *change identification.* Often without noticing, we take our place in a conversation. With the story of the adulterous woman, I almost never fail to line up with Jesus. After all, he will be bringing the redemptive word to the occasion—just as I will do, come Sunday morning with this text from John. On rare occasions I may identify with the woman—a sinner who found out that what she thought was her last day turned out to be her first.

The men are another story altogether. They look mean, uncaring—planning on killing her and tricking him. I'll have no part of them. Well, maybe I *ought* to take my place in the circle with them, and *then ask* why we're here. If I do so—and defend myself in my usual style—I may tell you that as a religious leader, I must take a stand on the moral corruption that is ruining our society. I do take the Law seriously. If we do not abide by it, as a community we shall lose our moorings and hence our future. You can't be cavalier about these things.

Well, with such a new perspective, as a preacher, I may then notice that Jesus was not the one who first made the turn toward grace. It was the eldest male in the circle—who was the first to drop the stone and who then, by the way, walked away alone and, because he failed the Torah in public, probably lost the respect of the community as well.

It is particularly important for positioning oneself to be surprised to talk to people. *Conversations* early in the preparation stage are timely; later they tend to be pleas for confirmation. Lay lectionary study groups meeting, say, on Sunday evening and/or clergy groups on Monday morning provide the preacher with the possibility of a huge array of ideas different from one's own—which, unfortunately, may be why some are not interested in this option. Such groups whet the appetite for views not noticed.

In particular, I have often been called upon to preside at such groups of clergy. Sometimes, my preview into the lectionary pericopes clearly spells doom for the "learning moment." I can sense that nothing there is worth talking about. That is, until I arrive with my idea and a half (which takes only a few minutes to survive). But then the group starts its conversation, and I am amazed at the terrific ideas. It is both a humbling and an incredibly enriching time. Sometimes in the case of a narrative text, a role-play can be particularly engaging with the group.

Imaginative *word-association exercises* can be mind-expanding experiences. Two kinds are worth noting. The first is to write a single word on a blank piece of paper—a word central to the text. Begin writing other words—any words that come to mind. Connect them with others; reverse them; alter them; modify them. Check for strange connections between words at the corners of the page. The point is not to review them—at the time, never veto them. To think of them is enough for them to be listed. The result is the kind of juxtaposition about which Paul Scott Wilson has already been cited. Recall he spoke of the "bringing together of two ideas that might not otherwise be connected and developing the creative energy they generate."[248] Such stimulating exercises are taught in the creative work *Writing the Natural Way* by Gabrielle Rico.[249]

The other form of such an exercise in the early stage of sermon preparation is to follow through on the often witnessed preacher's nightmare. Perhaps you have had the experience. You dream that it is time for you to move to the pulpit for the morning message. But you have not prepared. All you can do is read the text—which you know because you can find it on the back of the Sunday morning bulletin. So you read the text and wing it—in the dream. But sometimes it is a helpful daytime exercise, not a nightmare.

This can be an effective sermon preparation exercise, particularly when the text seems so unlikely a source for preaching. So when it becomes clear that nothing helpful is happening, just stand up, read the text, and start talking. Make sure you have pencil and paper handy, for you may be surprised at what comes out of the chaos of such free association.

Sometimes the word-association experience may consist of noticing other biblical texts that also deal with the theme of the text with which one is working. Although this is sometimes done in a proof-text way of supplying increased clout for the text, what I have in mind is quite different. I have in mind thinking about texts that say things differently—indeed, that may bring conflict to the text with which one is working.

But I think the most important behavior to engage for the sake of positioning oneself to be surprised has to do with *preparation timing*. I am presuming here that most of us utilize several different sittings or pacings in our sermon preparation—not just one. Preparation timing has to do with how we leave one session in order to reenter it at a later time.

Suppose you quit work on Tuesday afternoon and plan to return again on Thursday. Well, how you leave the Tuesday afternoon session is remarkably important. Perhaps you can recall the experience. You felt pretty good about the sermon-to-be late Tuesday afternoon—but upon returning Thursday, the notes were flat and the reentry almost impossible. It took forever to get going again. And you wondered why you felt so good about it earlier. There may be an easy explanation for the difficulty.

You may have left your preparation work on Tuesday at some point of closure. Perhaps you mused that the first part is now complete—and the second portion can be engaged later. Because you stopped work at the point of closure—entering the dead silence that follows Kermode's "tock"—your preconscious mind had nothing to ruminate about while you were busy doing other forms of ministry, engaging in family activities, and even sleeping.

Now, recall the opposite experience. You leave Tuesday afternoon sermon work very frustrated. Some aspects of the work went all right, but you could not solve one obstacle of thought. Finally, you decided to leave it for a while—actually until you return to the preparation on Thursday. When that time arrives, your mind engages quickly, energy is high, and somehow that obstacle is more malleable now. Of course, because while you were thinking about other matters for almost two days, your preconscious mind was not only hard at work, but playfully at work as well.

Why is it that we wake up in the middle of the night with our best insights? How can it be that all the good ideas happen in the shower where there is no yellow pad on which to write? The reason is that our conscious sermon preparation time involves obviously deliberate concentration. And like trying to remember a name, sometimes the more you work at it, the less you get. Besides, our finely honed theological-biblical principles are working with precision. Our minds know the truth and will not allow a single heretical thought for even a moment. Things are solid and safe—and not very creative.

But when you drop your conscious intentionality in order to do something else—a hospital call, a game of tennis, whatever—your preconscious mind is let loose, without such tight parameters of control. So, while you sleep, you really are still working on that sermon—only in a different mode. Is there any wonder that in that free-floating consciousness immediately prior to or after sleep the mind is fertile and ideas may rush? (Rollo May discusses how this happened in his life in his marvelous *The Courage to Create*.)[250]

All of which is to say that it is vital to conclude one session of sermon preparation work at the point of a *felt difficulty* (the active silence following Kermode's tick)—not at the point of closure. The mind will work on the sermon without the rigid constraints of conscious commitments. I recall once after I made this point in a workshop session, a journalism major came up to me recalling how his professor of journalism instructed the class about lunch breaks at the daily newspaper. "When you must leave the article for the break, always leave the writing in the middle of a sentence." Exactly.

We have now completed our exploration of the first stage of sermon preparation, the *attending stage*—consisting of three specific steps:

1. Immersing oneself in the text.
2. Looking for trouble.
3. Positioning oneself to be surprised.

The three preliminary steps have in common an openness for the experience of the text, a committedly open alertness toward the strange, and a positioned hopefulness to hear. Theologically, these steps are predicated on the belief that God's Spirit may be better able to break into the context of the preacher's expectant wonderment—even confusion—than into the position of known certainties.

Imagining

These next three steps in the preparation of the sermon move into a modality characterized less by "waiting upon" and characterized more by "acting upon"—yet not anywhere close to any kind of closure about what Sunday's sermon might be like. It is a shift toward more intentionality about the facticity of Sunday next. In the *imagining stage* of sermon preparation—as it typically occurs—the preacher is becoming relationally strategic.

This shift from the mode of *attending* to the mode of *imagining* is surely parallel to other artistic endeavors. Ever so surely, the creative energy of the preacher begins to turn toward the fluidity of nascent possibilities for Sunday. Three steps can be identified.

4. *Naming Important Issues, Images, and Incidents*

Having read aloud the texts in different translations and paraphrases, even one's own, one can now ask, "What is going on here?" "What is happening?" Where before the preparation focused on specific trouble, now *common tendencies* of the passage are allowed to surface by being named. For example, in the lectionary sequence on Paul's letter to the Galatians, one can discover a recurring wave of thought, image, and story.

Paul is angry. (It does not take great research capabilities of historical or narrative criticism to draw this conclusion.) He doesn't even begin the letter with his usual thanks. The madder he gets, the faster the images fly—with angels, spies, and false believers. Then he settles down to tough argument about flesh and spirit and their proper sequence—with concepts of justification, works, promise, and inheritance.

For emphasis he draws upon stories—of Cephas and Abraham. The powerful story of his confrontation with Simon Peter in Antioch somehow doesn't make it into the lectionary, nor does his fit of hope for the circumcision party: "I wish those who unsettle you would castrate themselves!"[251] The lectionary mentality prefers his solid argument to his angry eloquence.

The point is that after the specificity of steps two and three, the preacher is now becoming strategic about the sensibility of the passage. What might be surfacing is Paul's relation to the church in Galatia—and implicitly the pastor in relation to the congregation who will gather Sunday for worship—including a sermon based on the Galatians letter.

It is timely now to recall Buttrick's advice to name not so much the text's point as much as to ask: "What is the passage trying to do?"[252] The moment the matter is put that way, we have a before, an after, and a process in between. Justo González and Catherine González caution us about our interpretation of any passage: "We are not to see it as a gem floating in a void, but rather place it in its historical setting and ask the question of the direction of God's action in that text."[253]

Or to change the illustrative text, if the scripture for next Sunday's sermon is the parable of the good Samaritan, we do well to heed Bartlett's reminder that it will not be possible to be adequate for the task "if we have no idea of the relationship of Jews to Samaritans in the first century."[254]

We note what is now happening to us. Having attended the text, having looked for trouble, and positioning ourselves to be surprised, we are confronted with an increasing number of questions for which we do not yet have answers. Moreover, this is beginning to happen even as we are more and more catching a glimpse of the congregation in the corner of our homiletical eye—the congregation for whose life this sermon is being prepared. This is not going to be some sterile academic exercise; a congregation is almost in view.

A kind of figure-ground juxtaposition is going on at this point. Right now the text is figure; Sunday's congregation is ground—yet ever present. The preacher is beginning to imagine sermon possibilities. Then the figure-ground reverses itself.

5. Ruminating Potential Connections

All of a sudden, the preacher's concentration shifts focus to the congregation. Now Sunday sermon is figure; text becomes ground. Very explicitly, the preacher begins listening to the various voices of congregation, culture, and liturgy. Where we are in the Christian year, for example, will make a profound difference in what emerges from the biblical text for Sunday.

What is happening here is congregational exegesis. There is no sermon yet—the preacher is trying to find a fit. Things have moved just beyond the stage of hunches and leanings toward potential connections.

At this point in our imagined typical process, it is difficult to define what is happening—much less attempt to teach what ought to be happening. Yet, it can be sensed immediately in the conversational patterns of preachers in the middle of discussing a text. Someone will say, "That'll preach." The mental gymnastics of the others in the circle says it all as they attempt to join in the juxtaposition of found connection—which gets experienced almost as an electrical charge of energy.

It happens in a couple of ways. Consider four variables: (1) itch, (2) scratch, (3) text, and (4) congregation. These are the variables roaming around. Sometimes an explicit textual itch—an issue—will become connected to an as yet implicit textual scratch. The preacher senses the energy and knows something is at work—something is now possible. The preacher knows long before being able to define it.

Sometimes it is the reverse—an explicit scratch with an implicit itch. Were a church musician to ask about potential hymns that might work for Sunday, likely, the preacher would have no idea yet. Sometimes either itch or scratch is named or found or perceived first in the context of the congregation and then noticed also in the text.

As indefinable as this moment is to describe, we are dealing here with what often is called "the homiletical mind." For some, it is intuitively easy; for others, it is difficult and must be cultivated, must be intended. I believe it has to do with capacity for metaphor and analogy—which in a flash can make a connection. And connection *is* the topic here. Not truth, not sermonic point, and not theme sentence. Rather, connection, gestalt, a moment of insight. Which is exactly the purpose of the word-association exercises described in step three. Some of us need help in making connections that have homiletical consequences. I believe that if it can be described, it can then be cultivated. We can learn intentionally what for another may be a gift.

Even after the preacher senses—even vaguely—that something is at work, there is so much left to do. Indeed, most of actual detailed naming and shaping is yet to happen. At this point we are imagining. And the deeper we go in our imagining, the clearer it becomes that the time is ripe to hit the books.

6. *Engaging and Consulting as Scholar in Residence*

Some may be surprised we have waited so long to engage in hard exegetical work. Certainly, consulting exegetical experts is mandatory for the responsible preacher. Waiting until now for such assistance is important because premature closure in preparation is fatal for the preaching event. In particular, the first stage of *attending* (which included the first three steps of immersing oneself in the text, looking for trouble, and positioning oneself to be surprised) is specifically calculated to lure the preacher toward openness and wonderment—even confusion—and not closure and certainty.

Of course, as scholar in residence you will want to move toward the help of expert opinion, but if you move too quickly, you are likely never to have a fresh thought on your own. Craddock says it beautifully: "After all, who is going to venture a thought or an interpretation when at the very same desk are six internationally known Bible scholars?"[255]

The issue is not just that we feel intimidated by the experts. It is also that their task is to close things down—to help people form conclusions. Explains Craddock: "When used at the proper time they are indispensable, but if too early opened, they take over. . . . They intrude themselves between the text and the preacher and begin explaining everything."[256] Such an attitude never lets the homiletical mind loose. Moreover, the experts are tempted as are we, only at a more profound level. We get into ideological hermeneutical ruts; theirs may sometimes become a ditch.

Some years ago, I went to an expert for help with the account of Jesus being asked whether it was right to pay taxes to Caesar. Jesus' concluding response was something like "Do what's right"—which, of course, is not an answer, but the question restated. But the expert took great lengths to explain how this was not a clever evasion on Jesus' part, that Jesus made it clear that it was not idolatrous to pay such a tax because of the benefits provided by the state, that people should pay the tax, and moreover why Jesus held this particular view regarding things. Maybe. (How the expert knew all this is not evident to me from the text.)

Then the expert noted in passing that the event of handing Jesus the coin that day must have occurred in the Gentile court, because coins with images on them were not allowed in the Temple proper. Maybe. Or is it possible that the expert might have missed an incredibly telling and powerfully revealing moment? What if . . . ? Maybe.

At any rate, the many wonderful publications of lectionary exegetical scholarship are both terrific and dangerous. When preachers move straight from reading the text to reading someone else's account of what the text means, they likely lose immersion, conflict, and surprise. The energy of juxtaposition and the scrambling to engage a confusion are lost. Could this be why we hear so many sermons that are lessons of explanation? ("Our text today involves several principles we will understand and follow.")

The experts are not a substitute for one's own biblical homework. They assist, but the preacher—the scholar in residence—is the expert in knowing how a particular passage and a particular congregation might relate together. This hard work always happens in context. The preacher stands facing the text in the name of the congregation and faces the congregation in the name of the text. Finally, the preacher does both in the middle of the liturgy. Note, too, this present task is not without playful anticipation and gracious surprise, particularly at this moment in the preparation process.

If you can imagine sermon preparation as a kind of improvisational jazz piece, you will get the sense of how important it is to allow the music to get sideways, conflicted, pulled away from its simple mooring. It sometimes feels as though the musicians either have forgotten what piece they are playing or have lost their way. But then comes the turn toward home with a quiet celebratory sense of release visible in the eyes of the musicians— and concluding, then, with a simple reprise. What a trip.

In our preparation, we already have intentionally released our grip on the known and allowed the itch to move farther toward chaos. But now we are ready with the help of experts to make our way toward shaping the sermon and, finally, to head toward home—the experience of the denouement in the presentation on Sunday. What a trip.

There is, of course, the opposite and equally unfortunate problem of ministers who engage in overly individualistic sermon preparation. Some preachers—who may be quite creative—seem never to find it necessary to consult anybody. Lone Ranger interpreters, González and González call them. They work alone—interested neither in congregational pericope study groups nor in expert witnesses out of our common tradition of scholarship in the church.

We need always to remember that having a wonderfully creative idea while engaging a text does not make it justified. We turn to experts in the discipline for confirmation of legitimacy or negation of a "wonderful" but untenable idea.

I hope we do not need to choose between dull, scholarly, instructive lecture-sermons and snappy, creative sound bites. So I say, let the imagination run loose for a while. But now as we are about to begin actually shaping the sermon, it is time for closure—born of both creativity and scholarship. One great result of significant imaginative preparation time is that when we then turn to our scholarly work, our minds are ready with questions born of actual confusion, and wonderments waiting expectantly for birthing resolution. Such work is heady in more senses than one.

Now that we are ready to move into the third and final stage of sermon preparation, it might be helpful to glance back at the musing, conflict, and even confusion of the first stage of *attending*, recall the beginning strategies of the second stage of *imagining*, and take a peek ahead at the final stage of *shaping:*

Attending

1. Immersing oneself in the text.
2. Looking for trouble.
3. Positioning oneself to be surprised.

Imagining

4. Naming important issues, images, and incidents.
5. Ruminating potential connections.
6. Engaging and consulting as scholar in residence.

Shaping

7. Naming sermon focus and strategy.
8. Recognizing the sudden shift and positioning the good news.
9. Planning the sermon process.
10. Naming the aim.

Shaping

Typically there are four steps to the process of actually shaping the sermon.

7. Naming Sermon Focus and Strategy

It is time to reap the benefits of previous work, the value of which may not have been readily apparent. Remember the task back in step four? It had to do with naming important issues, images, and incidents. Well, now the preacher gets to choose. Out of all the variables of the text—given all the intervening thought-fulness—what appears credibly pertinent? Given several possible issues, which one likely can work well for Sunday? Is there an image around which everything seems to revolve? Or a brief dialogue between Jesus and another person that is quite telling?

In naming the central sermonic focus for Sunday, note how different this is from the way many of us learned. I was taught to choose a central *theme*—to be named by a one-sentence proposi-tional statement. Such a theme or topic sentence focused on the *scratch* of the sermon—the final bottom-line conclusion. Contrari-wise, what I am suggesting is to name the central *itch*.

In both cases the discipline of centered—hence, limited—scope is the desired effect. My experience is, however, that when most people name the *answer*, quickly the mind stops working. Sub-sequent preparation then becomes for many a kind of final fill-in-the-blanks experience—with *this* consequence named, *that* ramification noted, and *these* responses called for.

What needs naming is an answer for the question: What is at stake here, the presenting difficulty that will take a sermon to work through? We are identifying that central issue that will carry us all through the sermon, not naming the final resolution on the other side.

A special reason why it is essential to be clear about the focus—as here defined—is that other theorists, other writers, also utilize the term *focus*, but mean "what the sermon aims to say," the "unifying theme of the sermon"[257]—that is, the resolution. It is crucial to hear the difference of meaning as utilized here. Here, *focus* means "issue"—itch, not concluding scratch.

Before pressing on, before pursuing the matters of focus and strategy further, a couple of concerns need to be noted in passing—lest confusion strikes unproductively.

When thinking about the central issue—the core focus—we are talking about our intentionally imposed limitation on Sunday's sermon. We cannot adequately deal with every possible important issue of a text. We make choices. To believe that most texts have only one point—only one central theme—or only one presenting issue is generally a large mistake.

That is why a preacher can return to the same lectionary pericope again in three years and not be ideologically constrained to preach the same sermon. Likely, the text is polysemic, the congregation is different in three years, and the world has shifted significantly. My now retired colleague Charles Baughman used to smile knowingly and say about the Hebrew Scripture: "You can dig deeply all your life and never empty the text of meaning."

The second notation in passing is that although I have with apparent boldness alleged a ten-step preparation process— plotted if you please—the steps obviously are more fluid than this schematic might seem to suggest. Indeed, it is sometimes the case that before heading toward expert consultation and hard exegetical research (step six), the sermon focus (our present step) may already have been grasped. While positioning ourselves to be surprised (step three), on occasion it just may have been that a gripping juxtaposition between text and congregation made the focus abundantly clear a lot sooner. Hence, my use of the term *typically*. That is why I have suggested three broad preparation stages of *attending, imagining,* and *shaping.* We are still talking typically, although seldom do these three stages shift position.

The other important decision at this stage of preparation is choosing from among the integrative strategy choices of *argument, image,* and *story.* By this time it should be clear that the sermonic movement essentially will be carried along primarily by logic movement, or by the shifting impact of image or images, or by the process of a story line.

Recall that Thielicke's sermon on the Pharisee and publican *story* was carried by his *logic.* The story line was present, but not dominant. (I have had a few students make a good case for believing that Thielicke's images were actually the determining variable.) Although one might expect that a sermon based on a biblical parable will likely utilize the strategy of story, and so on, it is not necessarily the case. Bartlett is right: "Not every powerful sermon on a parable will be narrative in form, and some sermons on fairly discursive passages by Paul will be full of story."[258]

8. *Recognizing the Sudden Shift and Positioning the Good News*

All along, the preacher has been listening closely to discern the twist, the sudden shift that forces everything to take a different route home. It may be a piece of striking logic, an image turned upside down, or the sudden bend in the story's road.

Sensing the sudden shift has been on the back burner all the while we have performed these other tasks. Without the sudden shift, the listeners are likely to get home before the preacher—a most unfortunate occurrence. Once the sudden shift is identified, the rest is remarkably simple (most of the time).

Consider the parable of the talents as found in Matthew 25:14-28—with one slave given five talents, one given two, and the third given one. There are several possible moments involving shifts of thought and image—all nominations for recognition as the sudden shift.

For example, once you notice the enormity of the money involved—five talents equal seventy-five years of earnings (or two lifetimes of work), two talents equal thirty years of earnings, and one talent equals fifteen years of wages. If you wonder why the third servant was nervous, just imagine how you would feel walking about with fifteen years of your earnings in your pocket (that's way over $100,000 at minimum wage today). We're talking cash here. Personally, I'd look for a hiding place for it, wouldn't you?

Then Jesus had the owner say to all of them: Enter into the joy of the master. Which turns out a bit difficult since each servant began with zero capital, was lent some money, and then turned it all back plus all the earnings—to be left with zero capital once more. No profit whatever. Certainly, the owner is "full of joy" here. Why not? Even the third slave didn't gamble at Powerball with his portion—and the owner lost not one cent. "You shall have abundance." Pray tell, abundance of what? It turns out the answer is: abundance of work. That's the way it is. Work hard with a small assignment, and do well—and guess what's in store for you? Abundance.

Any of these observations could prompt selection as the sudden shift of thought. But the one that came to me happened while I was looking for good news in this bad news story. It never occurred to me while reading the RSV, which uses the term "servants." That is a euphemism. The NRSV comes right out with it: "slave." These are slaves. No wonder they didn't own anything first, middle, or last.

But note also how the story turns the whole world upside down. In a master-slave relation, the master has all the power; the slave gets all the vulnerability. That's how the system works. Except when this particular master headed off on his trip. Mind you, he didn't bring forward a little extra cash to keep the slaves happily occupied. He "entrusted his property to them"—that's what it says. He turned it all over to the slaves and headed on down the road. He didn't have to. He chose to.

Now then, during his absence, who has the power and the vulnerability? One can imagine the owner's nervousness on the way home because everything that he has and is and will be totally depends on what the slaves have done with who he is. It is called the grace of the gospel, that reverses the way the world works.

Once this moment is perceived as the sudden shift for this particular sermon, it likewise becomes clear that the gospel and the sudden shift come together at the same moment. Hence, such a sermon might commence with conflict (of their risk, perhaps) through complication (the owner's joy and their work) to the sudden shift (power and vulnerability reversal) to unfolding (there is joy after all—the joy of communion with a vulnerable master).

In the sermon as I preached it, what carried the movement, seems to me, was not the story line as such—although it was important. It was the series of shifting indelible images: cash in pocket, hole in ground, work as reward, slaves and master, reversal of roles, joy of communion, trust, and vulnerability.

9. Planning the Sermon Process

Once the previous step is taken in naming and planning the sudden shift and the related good news, the rest begins to fall into place. With this illustration still in our minds, it is now easier to speak of the relation of good news to the sudden shift. Speaking about the sudden shift seizes the notion of movement, sequence, and surprise. Talking about the good news concerns the announcement, the content, the event, the power of the gospel that is the flesh of the sermonic movement. Both are related to the unity of form and substance but come from opposite poles. Sometimes the sudden shift opens the door to the announcement of the gospel. Sometimes the gospel opens the door to the sudden shift. Sometimes—as in the case of our illustration—they happen together.

Clearly, the understanding of plotted movement—conflict, complication, sudden shift, and unfolding—provides the rationale for determining the placement of all the sermonic material. For example, no one would want to ruin the shock of the owner's vulnerability by prefacing the sermon with: "Welcome to this story about this wonderful master who risked everything he had in order to care for his servants." No. No.

Notice, for example, how the "plotting mentality" helps decide the crucial issue of where to place the text within the sermon itself. We recall the first stage of the sermon preparation process: (1) immersing oneself in the text, (2) looking for trouble, and (3) positioning oneself to be surprised. During these preliminary steps, it begins to become clear that the text is likely going to be part of the sermonic *itch* or part of the concluding sermonic *scratch* or something in between. If the text is all "answer," begin looking for trouble before the text itself. By the time we completed the second major stage of (4) naming issues, (5) ruminating connections, and (6) engaging as scholar in residence, we became ready to name the sermon focus and strategy. Once named, options for placement of the text become clear.

For example, the text may have been a parable of Jesus—in which case the text will lead the preacher and the congregation along their journey. The role of the preacher may be to *run the text*—amplifying here and there to the desired resolution or unfolding. On the other hand, there are times when the text is all affirmation—perhaps some glorious song of confidence in the power of the gospel. If so, it is quite possible that the text may not appear in the sermon as preached until quite late. It may constitute the sudden shift close to the end of the sermon. In this case, one might imagine the sermon beginning, not in the biblical world at all, but in the contemporary world of the parish. In this case, one might *delay the text* until the appropriate place in the plot.

Then again, sometimes a text is introduced early on, because it helps define the basic conflict that will be engaged on Sunday morning. But then, something blocks the text from achieving the sudden shift and final resolution. In such a case the preacher may want to *suspend the text* while hunting for something to unlock the way for the sudden shift and good news.

In the sermon text we have just been examining, the parable of the talents, this was my strategy. There is so much about the text that on the surface feels like bad news, that I chose to allow that assumption to grow in the sermon process as preached. I noted that the slaves had nothing of their own. Moreover, their work was all for the joy of the master, and worse yet, their only reward for duty accomplished was more work. I even wondered aloud if perhaps the third slave was not better off than the first—at least the third slave's work was complete. Then after things became as conflicted, as complicated as I could present them, I begged the text for some good news. Only then did I introduce the issue of the system of slavery and how the master had overturned the world's system—becoming intentionally vulnerable and hence evoking a shared communion that finally becomes the joy of the master and of everyone else.

There are other options, of course, the selection of which may prove difficult in some sermons. (I have dealt with this matter of placement of text selection in greater detail elsewhere.)[259] But the principle is clear. The strategy is not difficult to understand. We all utilized it as children in the games we played—even in the selection of the animals that occupied our imaginary backyard jungle. Nobody had to instruct us to place lions and tigers there and not cocker spaniels. Conflict and complication demanded it.

So it is that once the notion becomes clear that we are strategizing a plot-to-be—working from itch to scratch—the rationality takes over. By contrast, I remember—back when I was a topical deductive preacher—spending inordinate amounts of time trying to decide which of three points ought to come first: "Begin with the close at hand?" "Start with the longest point?" "Begin with the most explicitly theological?" Sometimes it all seemed rather arbitrary. But if I move *forward*—conflict, complication, sudden shift, and unfolding, in that order—then I have a rationale by which to make my decisions of shape.

10. Naming the Aim

It is not enough to be able to identify the content or issue or theme of a sermon. The question, finally, for every preacher every Sunday is: What do I hope will happen as a result of this sermon having been preached? Henry Mitchell speaks about the behavioral goals of experience and celebration, not just an ideational goal alone.[260]

Our task is, finally, to prompt, to evoke. We do not have the power to cause to be, but we are able to set the stage or, as my pastor friend Jud Souers put it, to pull back the curtain so that people might get a glimpse of the play.

Naming the aim is just about the last thing one does in sermon preparation—save prayer. If named too early in the preparation process, it gets in the way. Indeed, the sermon may have more in mind than we know early on. Some of our best sermons pulled a significant shift of purpose on us while we were yet preparing. The Spirit may yet change our minds. H. Grady Davis's sermonic "tree" may grow differently from what we expected at first. It does have a life of its own. The sermon's aim should be named only after other preparation is complete.

On the other hand, if the aim cannot finally be stated late, late Saturday night, sermon preparation likely is not quite finished. Naming the aim is the test of profound clarity. If we cannot name it, it may not be clear—yet.

This does not intend, however, a reductionism to some narrow prosaic truth that can be understood or explained in quick problem-solution modality. Indeed, there is a difference between the *indefinite* and the *mystery*. The *poetic* does not signal the *vague*. When we are dancing the edge of mystery, we need to know where we are and hence where and how the mystery might be approached.

Although the mystery cannot be captured by our endeavors, our gestures toward it must be credibly clear, pointed, and evocative. After all, the evocation is our proper and sacred task; the Word proclaimed is, then, left in God's hands. We will do our best to facilitate it; when it happens, we are among the graced.

Sunday. Sunday comes and the people of God arrive for another little Easter. It is a family reunion taking place here—resembling in significant ways another kind of family reunion I have understood for years. Our particular clan gathers each year on the third Sunday of August. Some of the folks I do not know and some are really "not my kind," but we exchange friendly glances and a polite nod. Others I love deeply.

In one sense the variety of subjective responses does not matter. After all, we did not choose each other to begin with—we got chosen. We come not to a recollection, but to a reunion. We come to regroup, to break bread and rehearse the stories again. We gather to become who we are, and to be sent into the world with a name once more.

Well, Abraham and Sarah are kin, too, and James and John and Mary and Martha. When the family of God gathers each week for its reunion, some of our relatives we scarcely know. Others may not be particularly likable folk. But we *are* kin, even the strangers. We share a history and mutually carry a name and a claim. The hymns we sing together connect us more deeply than we are able to say. We are bonded again by prayer and creed and sacrament.

In this context it is time for the preacher to "bring the morning message." In the plot called liturgy comes the subplot called sermon. It is not only the case that "faith comes from what is heard,"[261] faith also is nurtured, challenged, confirmed from hearing—whether that hearing moves directly from mouth to ear, or from mouth through ear to signing hand to eye. It is an oral-aural experience, quite different from literality. As theologian Tom Driver once put it: "Ritual loves not paper."[262]

Even the Book arose out of the context of orality. Joanna Dewey makes the claim that the Gospel of Mark reveals "the legacy of orality," that "its methods of composition are primarily oral,"[263] and even "composed for a listening rather than a reading audience."[264] Walter Ong speaks of the Bible as having "massive oral underpinnings."[265] So, when we get up to preach, we need to honor the medium in which we work. Sometimes it has not come easily.

"Perhaps the single biggest failure in the teaching of preaching," comments Robin Meyers, "is that young ministers are not fully impressed with the difference between textuality and orality." He explains that "shaped by mountains of books, called upon to write scores of papers, and graded largely by what they commit to the page, aspiring preachers train the eye but neglect the ear"—in spite of the fact that "it is into the world of sound that they will go, plying their wares acoustically."[266] (Sometimes we divert the power of sound by asking people to look at a pew Bible for the reading of the text.)

Tex Sample reminds us that while the life of the church requires literality, it also must utilize orality—"finding the way to be concretely life-based with people who may very well make up the majority of its members."[267] Undergirding Meyers' point of view, Sample has remarked repeatedly that often by the time people graduate from seminary, they have become unfit to relate to the vast number of people who live most of their lives in the mode of orality.

Might this relate to what John Holbert meant when he spoke of a "White middle class church . . . leadership [that] has been taught to scoff at . . . the . . . world view of the average member"?[268]

Frankly, I believe this problem is beginning to be addressed in our time. The North American preaching models that comprise what some call "the New Homiletic" are committed to the mode of sound that places us, as Ong puts it, "in the middle of actuality and in simultaneity."[269] "Spoken words are events," he explains, "engaged in time and indeed in the present."[270] Moreover, "sound unites groups of living beings as nothing else does." Henry Mitchell speaks of how the black church in North America has helped maintain the "primacy of the oral"—a tradition that is "actually the early church's method."[271]

Perhaps that is why in spite of admitting its accuracy, I always flinch when we speak of "writing a sermon." Clearly, there is some adverse mix of media implicit in that phrase—seems to me. I can remember years in parish ministry when my plotted sermons were nonetheless prepared in full manuscript form. I tried—and to some degree successfully—to ensure the modality of orality by always writing the manuscript out loud. It has become a lifestyle for me—so much so that at this very moment of writing this book, I am speaking this line out loud.

The battle between manuscript—even prepared out loud—and the medium of orality, finally, for me was resolved by my discarding not only the manuscript, but even extensive notes. I generally carry a four-by-six card into the pulpit—in case of emergency. Whether by manuscripts or a few notes, orality is a different form of communication from that of print. The sentences are constructed differently; repetition has a totally different purpose and style; even the grammar shifts. And community is established.

For years now, I have found the work of Clyde Fant extremely helpful, as he teaches us how to prepare what he calls "the oral manuscript."[272] He believes that preparation should occur "in the medium which will eventually be used."[273] The result is a "sermon brief," in which "key directional sentences" introduce a "thought block."[274] After all, he reasons, we do not speak in paragraphs; we speak in sections or blocks of thought.

Tom Troeger says it magnificently when he calls us to "listen to the music of speech." He explains: "The physical properties of speech—its rhythm, pitch, volume, and inflection—are a kind of music that makes the imagination dance."[275] Moreover, there is a "melody of words" that engages us in spoken speech. The lift, the lilt, the beat, the intensities, and the softenings of speech convey the truth that is forever greater than our words."[276] Even when Troeger uses a manuscript, he images it "as a musical score."[277] No wonder the "voice of the preacher . . . [becomes] an aural symbol, just as the chalice, the altar, and the cross are visual symbols."[278]

The notion of one's manuscript or notes functioning like a musical score underscores (shall we say) the possibility of evocation. "The preacher's voice uses words and the physical properties of sound to draw people beyond the message that is being articulated into the presence of God."[279]

Did you catch the key term here? To "draw people *beyond.*" And before that, a "truth that is forever greater than our words." To evoke, to pull the curtain back. The "score" accompanies a dance of orality that, like music, comes out of silence, is here now, and then moves on back into silence—while the presence of its memory dances. As Ong puts it: "The word as sound signals interiority and mystery."[280]

The sermon event happens. In the corporate act of worship, speech is gesturing toward the ineffable, and undulating sound waves are dancing the edge of mystery.

NOTES

1. Fred Craddock, *As One Without Authority* (Enid, Okla.: Phillips University, 1974), p. 1.
2. Ibid., p. 62.
3. Hans Frei, *The Eclipse of Biblical Narrative* (New Haven: Yale University Press, 1974).
4. Richard Eslinger, *A New Hearing* (Minneapolis: Fortress Press, 1995), p. 65.
5. H. Grady Davis, *Design for Preaching* (Philadelphia: Fortress Press, 1958), p. 15.
6. David Buttrick, *Homiletic* (Philadelphia: Fortress Press, 1987), p. 189.
7. David Buttrick, *A Captive Voice* (Louisville: Westminster/John Knox Press, 1994), p. 80.
8. David Buttrick, "Interpretation and Preaching," *Interpretation* Vol. 35 (January 1981): 49.
9. Buttrick, *Captive Voice*, p. 81.
10. Frei, *Eclipse*, p. 27.
11. Ibid., p. 130.
12. Mark Ellingsen, *The Integrity of Biblical Narrative* (Minneapolis: Fortress, 1990), p. 11.
13. Henry H. Mitchell, *The Recovery of Preaching* (San Francisco: Harper & Row, 1977), p. 12.
14. Ibid., p. 13.
15. Thomas G. Long, "And How Shall They Hear?" in *Listening to the Word*, ed. Gail R. O'Day and Thomas G. Long (Nashville: Abingdon Press, 1993), p. 170.
16. Ibid., pp. 172-74.
17. Ibid., p. 177.
18. Craddock, *As One*, p. 67.
19. Ibid., p. 55.
20. Ibid., p. 124.
21. Ibid., p. 62.
22. Stephen Cites "The Narrative Quality of Experience," in *Why Narrative?* ed. Stanley Hauerwas and L. Gregory Jones (Grand Rapids: Eerdmans, 1989), p. 67.
23. Frederick Jameson, "Sartre: The Origins of Style," in *Time and Reality: Studies in Contemporary Fiction*, ed. Margaret Church (Chapel Hill: University of North Carolina Press, 1949), p. 260.
24. Thomas Mann "The Magic Mountain," in *Time and Western Man*, ed. Wyndham Lewis. (Boston: Beacon Press, 1957), p. 131.
25. Hauerwas and Jones, *Why Narrative?*, p. 66.
26. Terrence W. Tilley, *Story Theology* (Wilmington, Del.: Michael Glazier, 1985), p. 24.
27. Lonnie D. Kliever, *The Shattered Spectrum* (Atlanta: John Knox Press, 1981), p. 156.
28. Eugene L. Lowry, *Doing Time in the Pulpit* (Nashville: Abingdon Press, 1985), p. 8.
29. Richard L. Eslinger, *Narrative and Imagination* (Minneapolis: Fortress Press, 1995), p. 7.
30. Robert Reid, Jeffrey Bullock, and David Fleer, "Preaching as the Creation of an Experience: the Not-So-Rational Revolution of the New Homiletic," *The Journal of Communication and Religion* 18, no. 1 (March 1995): 1.

31. David Buttrick, "On Doing Homiletics Today," in *Intersections: Post-Critical Studies in Preaching,* ed. Richard L. Eslinger (Grand Rapids, Mich.: Eerdmans, 1994), p. 89.
32. Ibid., p. 94.
33. Paul Scott Wilson, *The Practice of Preaching* (Nashville: Abingdon Press, 1995), p. 12.
34. Lucy Atkinson Rose, "Preaching in the Round-Table Church," Ph.D. dissert. (Graduate School of Emory University, 1994).
35. Ibid., p. 116.
36. Robert Stephen Reid, "Postmodernism and the Function of the New Homiletic in Post-Christendom Congregations," *Homiletic* 20, no. 2 (Winter 1995): 1.
37. Craddock, *As One,* p. 54.
38. Ibid., p. 60.
39. Ibid., p. 52.
40. Ibid., p. 56.
41. Ibid., p. 62.
42. Craddock, *Overhearing the Gospel* (Nashville: Abingdon, 1978), p. 137.
43. Toni Craven, "An Introduction to Narrative" (a paper read at Society of Biblical Literature meeting, Irvine, Texas, March 16, 1996), p. 4.
44. Rose, "Preaching in the Round-Table Church," p. 153.
45. Eugene L. Lowry, "Narrative Preaching," in *Concise Encyclopedia of Preaching,* ed. William H. Willimon and Richard Lischer (Louisville: Westminster/John Knox Press, 1995), p. 342.
46. Mitchell, *Recovery of Preaching,* p. 29.
47. Ibid., p. 32.
48. William B. McClain, *Come Sunday: The Liturgy of Zion* (Nashville: Abingdon Press, 1990), pp. 67-68.
49. Evans E. Crawford, *The Hum* (Nashville: Abingdon Press, 1995), p. 31.
50. McClain, *Come Sunday,* p. 68.
51. Ibid., p. 69.
52. Mitchell, *Recovery of Preaching,* p. 35.
53. Ibid., p. 58.
54. Buttrick, *Homiletic,* p. 333.
55. Ibid., p. 334.
56. Ibid., p. 362.
57. Ibid., p. 367.
58. Ibid., p. 405.
59. Buttrick, *Captive Voice,* p. 131.
60. Buttrick, *Homiletic,* pp. 292-93.
61. Buttrick, "On Doing Homiletics Today," in *Intersections,* p. 95.
62. Buttrick, "Interpretation and Preaching," p. 54
63. O'Day and Long, *Listening to the Word,* pp. 99-100.
64. Carol M. Norén, *The Woman in the Pulpit* (Nashville: Abingdon Press, 1991), p. 130.
65. Ibid., p. 155.
66. Lucy Rose, "Conversational Preaching: A Proposal," in *Papers of the Annual Meeting of the Academy of Homiletics* (Atlanta: November 30–December 2, 1995), p. 34.
67. Norén, *Woman in the Pulpit,* p. 96.
68. Ibid., p. 94.
69. Paul Scherer, *The Word God Sent* (New York: Harper & Row, 1965), p. 72.
70. Ibid., p. 23.
71. Ibid., p. 24.
72. Ibid., p. 25.
73. Barbara Brown Taylor, *The Preaching Life* (Cambridge: Cowley Publications, 1993), p. 77.
74. Frederick Buechner, *Telling the Truth* (New York: Harper & Row, 1977), pp. 16-17.
75. Craddock, *Preaching,* (Nashville: Abingdon Press, 1985), p. 52.
76. Charles L. Rice, *Interpretation and Imagination* (Philadelphia: Fortress Press, 1970), p. 15.
77. Rose, "Preaching in the Round-Table Church."
78. James William Cox, *Preaching* (San Francisco: Harper & Row, 1985), p. ix.
79. John A. Broadus and Jesse Burton Weatherspoon, *On the Preparation and Delivery of Sermons* (New York: Harper & Brothers, 1944), p. 244.

80. Buttrick, "On Doing Homiletics Today," p. 103.
81. Karl Barth, *Homiletics* (Louisville: Westminster/John Knox Press, 1991), p. 118.
82. Ibid., p. 119.
83. Karl Barth, *The Word of God and the Word of Man* (New York: Harper & Brothers, 1957), pp. 124-25.
84. Pauline Marie Rosenau, *Post-Modernism and the Social Sciences* (Princeton: Princeton University Press, 1992), pp. 169-76.
85. Lucy Rose, "The Parameters of Narrative Preaching," *Journeys Toward Narrative Preaching,* ed. Wayne Bradley Robinson (New York: Pilgrim Press, 1990), pp. 24-47.
86. Rose, "Preaching in the Round-Table Church," pp. 176-238.
87. Harry Emerson Fosdick, *The Living of These Days* (New York: Harper & Brothers, 1956), pp. 99-100.
88. Gustaf Wingren, *The Living Word* (Philadelphia: Fortress Press, 1960), p. 108.
89. Buttrick, *Homiletic,* p. 456.
90. Ibid., p. 11.
91. Ibid., p. 261.
92. Ibid., p. 212.
93. Ibid., p. 213.
94. Ibid., p. 189.
95. Ibid., p. 253.
96. Paul Scott Wilson, *The Practice of Preaching* (Nashville: Abingdon Press, 1995), p. 21.
97. Ibid., p. 22.
98. Rose, "Conversational Preaching," p. 34.
99. Ibid., p. 37.
100. Dietrich Ritschl, *A Theology of Proclamation* (Richmond, Va.: John Knox Press, 1960), p. 21.
101. Taylor, *The Preaching Life,* p. 85.
102. Craddock, *Preaching,* p. 65.
103. James H. Cone, *God of the Oppressed* (New York: Seabury Press, 1975), p. 18.
104. Rebecca S. Chopp, *The Power to Speak* (New York: Crossroad Publishing Co., 1989), p. 32.
105. David James Randolph, *The Renewal of Preaching* (Philadelphia: Fortress, 1969), p. 19.
106. Thomas F. Green, *The Activities of Teaching* (New York: McGraw-Hill, 1971), pp. 137-45.
107. Robert E. C. Browne, *The Ministry of the Word* (Philadelphia: Fortress, 1958, 1975), p. 74.
108. David J. Schlafer, *Surviving the Sermon* (Cambridge: Cowley Publications, 1992), p. 29.
109. Buttrick, *Homiletic,* p. 189.
110. Ibid., p. 253.
111. Browne, *Ministry of the Word,* p. 80.
112. Ibid., p. 27.
113. Ibid., p. 28.
114. Ibid., p. 30.
115. Hendrikus Berkhof, *Christian Faith* (Grand Rapids, Mich.: Eerdmans, 1979), p. 53.
116. Chopp, *Power to Speak,* p. 5.
117. P. T. Forsyth, *Positive Preaching and the Modern Mind* (Grand Rapids, Mich.: Eerdmans, 1964), p. 53.
118. Ibid.
119. Arthur Van Seters, ed., *Preaching as a Social Act* (Nashville: Abingdon Press, 1988), p. 17.
120. Crites, "The Narrative Quality of Experience," pp. 79-80.
121. Van Seters, *Preaching as a Social Act,* p. 17.
122. Chopp, *Power to Speak,* p. 6.
123. Browne, *Ministry of the Word,* p. 15.
124. Davis, *Design for Preaching,* p. 19.
125. Gene M. Tucker, "Reading and Preaching the Old Testament," in *Listening to the Word,* p. 34.
126. Ellingsen, *Integrity of Biblical Narrative,* p. 63.
127. Ibid.
128. Walter Brueggemann, *Finally Comes the Poet* (Minneapolis: Fortress Press, 1989), p. 8.
129. Browne, *Ministry of the Word,* p. 70.
130. Ibid., p. 114.

131. Sallie McFague, *Speaking in Parables* (Philadelphia: Fortress Press, 1975), p. 93.
132. Browne, *Ministry of the Word*, p. 49.
133. McFague, *Speaking in Parables*, p. 50.
134. Ibid., p. 77.
135. Brueggemann, *Finally Comes the Poet*, p. 27.
136. Brown, *Ministry of the Word*, p. 68.
137. Brueggemann, *Finally Comes the Poet*, p. 27.
138. Robert Roth, *Story and Reality* (Grand Rapids, Mich.: Eerdmans, 1973), pp. 152, 164, 165.
139. Browne, *Ministry of the Word*, p. 44.
140. Tucker, "Reading and Preaching the Old Testament," p. 34.
141. Gary Comstock, "Truth or Meaning: Ricoeur versus Frei on Biblical Narrative," *Journal of Religion* 66 (1986): 121.
142. Mark Allan Powell, *What Is Narrative Criticism?* (Minneapolis: Fortress Press, 1990), p. 8.
143. David L. Bartlett, "Story and History: Narratives and Claims," *Interpretation* 45, no. 3 (July 1991): 232.
144. William C. Placher, *Unapologetic Theology* (Louisville: Westminster/John Knox Press, 1989), p. 161.
145. Comstock, "Truth or Meaning," p. 131.
146. Cited in Placher, *Unapologetic Theology*, p. 164.
147. Stanley Hauerwas and David Burrell, "From System to Story: An Alternative Pattern for Rationality in Ethics," in *Why Narrative?* p. 185.
148. Placher, *Unapologetic Theology*, p. 165.
149. Thomas H. Troeger, "A Poetics of the Pulpit for Post-Modern Times," in *Intersections*, p. 43.
150. Ibid., p. 62.
151. Placher, *Unapologetic Theology*, p. 12.
152. Comstock, "Truth or Meaning," p. 131.
153. Placher, *Unapologetic Theology*, p. 134.
154. Ibid., p. 130.
155. Craddock, *Preaching*, p. 65.
156. Davis, *Design for Preaching*, p. 41.
157. Ibid., p. 43.
158. Ibid., p. 21.
159. Taylor, *The Preaching Life*, p. 82.
160. Eliseo Vivas, *Creation and Discovery* (Chicago: Gateway Editions, Henry Regnery Co., 1955), p. 134.
161. Ibid., p. 160.
162. Robin R. Meyers, *With Ears to Hear* (Cleveland: Pilgrim Press, 1993), p. 122.
163. Paul Scott Wilson, *Imagination of the Heart* (Nashville: Abingdon Press, 1988), p. 171.
164. Thomas G. Long, "Edmund Steimle and the Shape of Contemporary Homiletics," *The Princeton Seminary Bulletin*, n.s., 11, no. 3 (1990): 257.
165. M. Eugene Boring in *Listening to the Word*, p. 54.
166. Long, in *Listening to the Word*, p. 255.
167. Craddock, *As One*, p. 151.
168. Buttrick, *Homiletic*, p. 294.
169. Frank Kermode, cited in Stephen D. Crites, "The Narrative Quality of Experience," *Journal of the American Academy of Religion* vol. 39 (September 1971): 306.
170. Lowry, "Narrative Preaching," p. 342.
171. Lowry, "The Revolution of Sermonic Shape," in *Listening to the Word*, pp. 93-112.
172. Lowry, *Doing Time in the Pulpit*.
173. McClain, *Come Sunday*, p. 69.
174. Buttrick, cited by Lowry in *Listening to the Word*, p. 99.
175. Buttrick, *Homiletic*, p. 24.
176. Ibid., p. 373.
177. Buttrick, "Interpretation and Preaching," p. 52.
178. Ibid., p. 54.
179. Edmund A. Steimle, Morris J. Niedenthal, and Charles L. Rice, *Preaching the Story* (Philadelphia: Fortress Press, 1980), p. 171.

180. Wilson, *Imagination of the Heart*, p. 32.
181. Ibid., p. 65.
182. Ibid., p. 66.
183. Cited in Eslinger, *Narrative and Imagination*, p. 67.
184. Buttrick, *Homiletic*, p. 120.
185. Rose, "Preaching in the Round-Table Church."
186. Steimle, Niedenthal, and Rice, *Preaching the Story*, p. 19.
187. Karl Barth, *The Word of God and the Word of Man*, p. 116.
188. Walter Brueggemann, *Finally Comes the Poet*, pp. 109-10.
189. Schlafer, *Surviving the Sermon*, p. 22.
190. Ibid., pp. 34-58.
191. Ibid., p. 59.
192. Luke 9:32 JB.
193. Brueggemann, *Finally Comes the Poet*, p. 45.
194. Leroy Ostransky, *The Anatomy of Jazz* (Seattle: University of Washington, 1960), p. 83.
195. Browne, *Ministry of the Word*, p. 17.
196. Eugene L. Lowry, *The Homiletical Plot* (Atlanta: John Knox Press, 1980), pp. 36-46.
197. Fred B. Craddock, "Amazing Grace," *Thesis Theological Cassettes 7*, no. 5.
198. Crawford, *The Hum*, p. 52.
199. Ibid., p. 50.
200. 1 Kings 19:12 NRSV.
201. Schlafer, *Surviving the Sermon*, pp. 59-76.
202. Ibid., p. 63.
203. Patricia Wilson-Kastner, *Imagery for Preaching* (Minneapolis: Fortress Press, 1989), p. 20.
204. Roth, *Story and Reality*, p. 52.
205. Lowry, *Homiletical Plot*, p. 47.
206. Lowry, *Doing Time in the Pulpit*, p. 74.
207. S. H. Butcher, ed., *Aristotle's Theory of Poetry and Fine Art* (New York: Dover, 1951), p. 41.
208. John Dominic Crossan, *In Parables* (New York: Harper & Row, 1973), pp. 37-120.
209. Amos N. Wilder, *Early Christian Rhetoric* (Cambridge, Mass.: Harvard University Press, 1964), p. 71.
210. Matthew 20:16 RSV.
211. Paraphrase of Matthew 16:25.
212. Luke 10:30-36.
213. Paraphrase of John 9:40.
214. Mark 10:46-52.
215. Galatians 3.
216. Mark 12:41-44.
217. Luke 4:1-13.
218. Wilson, *Imagination of the Heart*, p. 108.
219. Paraphrase of Matthew 19:27.
220. Craven, "An Introduction to Narrative," p. 6.
221. Ibid.
222. Gabriel Fackre, "Narrative Theology: An Overview" in *Interpretation* vol. 37 (October 1983): 343.
223. Craddock, *Preaching*, p. 160.
224. Helmut Thielicke, *The Waiting Father* (New York: Harper & Brothers, 1959), p. 131.
225. Ibid.
226. Romans 8:31a. NRSV
227. Romans 8:31b NRSV.
228. Brueggemann, *Finally Comes the Poet*, p. 43.
229. Ibid., p. 2.
230. Romans 8:32 NRSV.
231. Browne, *Ministry of the Word*, p. 41.
232. Brueggemann, *Finally Comes the Poet*, p. 3.
233. Romans 8:35 NRSV.
234. Romans 8:37 NRSV.

235. Brueggemann, *Finally Comes the Poet*, p. 4.
236. Romans 12:1a NRSV.
237. Schlafer, "Living with the Lectionary," handout to accompany working paper at seminar (College of Preachers, Washington, D.C., June 1995, mimeographed).
238. Vivas, *Creation and Discovery*, p. 146.
239. Brueggemann, *Finally Comes the Poet*, p. 109.
240. Luke 1:4 NRSV.
241. Bartlett, "Story and History," p. 229.
242. Jeff Stein, ed., *The Random House Dictionary of the English Language* (New York: Random House, 1977), p. 298.
243. David L. Bartlett, "Texts Shaping Sermons," *Listening to the Word*, p. 158.
244. James L. Adams, *Conceptual Blockbusting* (San Francisco: W. H. Freeman & Co., 1974), p. 24.
245. Luke 12:13-21 NRSV.
246. Matthew 6:34 NRSV.
247. Joel Arthur Barker, *Future Edge* (New York: William Morrow & Co., 1992), pp. 157-58.
248. Wilson, *Imagination of the Heart*, p. 32.
249. Gabrielle Rico, *Writing the Natural Way* (New York: J. B. Tarcher, Putnam Publishing Group, 1983).
250. Rollo May, *The Courage to Create* (New York: W. W. Norton, 1975).
251. Galatians 5:12 NRSV.
252. Buttrick, "Interpretation and Preaching," p. 54.
253. Justo L. González and Catherine Gunsalus González, *Liberation Preaching* (Nashville: Abingdon Press, 1980), p. 84.
254. Bartlett, "Story and History," p. 232.
255. Craddock, *Preaching*, p. 106.
256. Ibid.
257. Thomas G. Long, *The Witness of Preaching* (Louisville: Westminster/John Knox Press, 1989), p. 86.
258. Bartlett, *Listening to the Word*, p. 149.
259. Eugene L. Lowry, *How to Preach a Parable* (Nashville: Abingdon Press, 1989).
260. Mitchell, *Recovery of Preaching*, pp. 30-73.
261. Romans 10:17 NRSV.
262. Tom F. Driver, *The Magic of Ritual: Our Need for Liberating Rites that Transform Our Lives and Our Communities* (San Francisco: Harper SF, 1991), p. 218.
263. Joanna Dewey, "Oral Methods of Structuring Narrative in Mark," in *Intersections*, p. 23.
264. Ibid., p. 35.
265. Walter J. Ong, S. J., *The Presence of the Word* (New Haven: Yale University, 1967), p. 21.
266. Robin R. Meyers, *With Ears to Hear* (Cleveland, Ohio: Pilgrim Press, 1993), p. 21.
267. Tex Sample, *Ministry in an Oral Culture: Living with Will Rogers, Uncle Remus, and Minnie Pearl* (Louisville: Westminster/John Knox Press, 1994), p. 22.
268. John C. Holbert, *Preaching Old Testament* (Nashville: Abingdon Press, 1991), p. 37.
269. Ong, *Presence of the Word*, p. 128.
270. Ibid., p. 34.
271. Mitchell, *Recovery of Preaching*, p. 75.
272. Clyde E. Fant, *Preaching for Today* (New York: Harper & Row, 1975), p. 118.
273. Ibid., p. 120.
274. Ibid., p. 122.
275. Thomas H. Troeger, *Imagining a Sermon* (Nashville: Abingdon Press, 1990), p. 67.
276. Ibid., p. 68.
277. Ibid., p. 76.
278. Ibid., p. 71.
279. Ibid.
280. Ong, *Presence of the Word*, p. 314.

INDEX

Printed in the United States
86496LV00007B/319-360/A

9 780687 015436